The Open University
Arts: A Second Level Course
The Enlightenment

Unit 6
Architecture and Landscape

Prepared for the Course Team by Colin Cunningham and Gillian Perry

Chiswick House, London, plan of the garden and views of the garden buildings, by J. Rocque, 1736. (Detail, complete plan illustrated as figure 32). Reproduced by permission of the Syndics of the Cambridge University Library.

The Open University Press

The Open University Press
Walton Hall, Milton Keynes
MK7 6AA

First published 1980. Reprinted 1983.

Designed by the Graphic Design Group of the Open University

Typeset by Santype International Ltd, Salisbury, Wilts, and printed in Great Britain by Waterlow Ltd., Member of the BPCC Group.

ISBN 0 335 07603 3

This text forms part of an Open University course. The complete list of units in the course appears at the end of this text.

For general availability of supporting material referred to in this text, please write to Open University Educational Enterprises Limited, 12 Cofferidge Close, Stony Stratford, Milton Keynes, MK11 1BY, Great Britain.

Further information on Open University courses may be obtained from the Admissions Office, The Open University, P.O. Box 48, Walton Hall, Milton Keynes, MK7 6AB.

1.2

Contents

Study material

You will need to refer to the Course Anthology, *The Age of Enlightenment: An Anthology of Eighteenth-century Texts*, edited by Simon Eliot and Beverley Stern (1979), Ward Lock Educational, and to the A204 *Colour Booklet* and *Gazetteer*. Volume 2 of the Course Anthology contains suggested ancillary reading: articles and extracts from Batty Langley, Laugier, Horace Walpole and Sir Joshua Reynolds. The *Colour Booklet* contains those illustrations designated as 'plates' in this unit and the *Gazetteer* is a guide to important eighteenth-century buildings and collections of eighteenth-century art in the British Isles and also contains a glossary of art historical terms.

Television programme 2 'Bath: A Theatre for Pleasure and Intrigue' shows the relationship between the architecture and the city of Bath; television programme 3 'A Little Gothick Castle' is concerned with Walpole's pioneering venture at Strawberry Hill, Twickenham. Radio programme 6 'Batty Langley' is a radiovision programme presented by Sir John Summerson and discusses pattern books for craftsmen.

Aim

The aim of this unit, which is in two parts, is to enable you to understand and enjoy aspects of the architecture and art of the period covered by the course. If this period is sometimes called the age of enlightenment, it is also known as the age of elegance; the buildings we have selected and the work of Thomas Gainsborough fully reflect this. Though there is a strong theoretical basis for much of the architecture and painting, they are not always directly linked to the currents of thought of the time. Nevertheless the houses and paintings you will study are part of the visible background against which should be set the works of the literary and intellectual elite you will meet elsewhere in the course. Contemporary ideas did influence artists and architects, as they influenced their patrons, but such connections often work both ways, and in any case we felt it more important to study and enjoy these works in their own right than to try to find in them any clear-cut 'enlightenment' theories. They are after all a vital part of the eighteenth-century social scene.

Part 1 Architecture in the Age of Reason

Introduction

The aim of Part 1 is to introduce you to the British architectural practices of the eighteenth century and to provide you with the necessary architectural language to enable you to study and enjoy the country houses that are some of the best loved creations of Georgian building. I want you to understand the artistic and architectural bases of the designs, to see how the styles developed as the century progressed and to be aware of how these houses answered the needs and formed the setting for the class that built them.

I have decided to concentrate on country houses because they reflect so many of the aspirations of the eighteenth-century gentry, but don't forget that in doing so I am deliberately ignoring whole areas and many key buildings. Church building, university and government architecture were all important and the period from 1720 to 1760 saw the birth of town planning in this country. You will see something of this in television programme 2, on Bath, and you should also try to watch television programme 3, which discusses the very unusual house built for Horace Walpole at Strawberry Hill. There was also a vast expansion in small Georgian houses for the middle classes, which followed on a simpler scale the conventions and styles of the nobility.

The material is not arranged as a single chronological development but presents the material in three stages: Section 1 contains an outline of the period; Sections 2 and 3 set the architecture in context and introduce some of the characters involved. The main developments are presented in more detail in Section 4, which concentrates on the theoretical basis, and Section 5 then re-examines the same themes introducing more technical detail. The case studies allow you to practise skills developed in the earlier sections.

1 The Development of British Architecture in the Eighteenth Century

The period from about 1715 to 1790 was the era in which Georgian architecture swept the board, establishing canons of good taste that are valued still for their essentially human scale and elegance. During the whole of that time the dominant style was classical, a dress that could be elaborated for the grandest palace or echoed in the simplest doorcase of a terrace house (fig 1).

Figure 1 Small Georgian house doorway, Worcester, *c* 1804. Photograph Colin Cunningham.

The main development began with the rejection of English baroque and the almost total dominance of the severe *Palladian* style, epitomized by the work of Colen Campbell (1676–1729) (see fig 6), William Kent (1685–1748) and Roger Morris (1695–1749). Other architects such as James Gibbs (1682–1754) (*Gazetteer* no 6) and Giacomo Leoni (*c* 1686–1746) (*Gazetteer* no 34) introduced a more individual or flamboyant note, but in the hands of a second generation[1] Palladianism remained

[1] The principal Palladian architects of the second generation were James Paine (*c* 1717–89), Robert Taylor (1714–88) and John Carr of York (1723–1807).

the main force until about 1750 (*Gazetteer* no 19). Thereafter the rigid Palladian style developed into a more varied *Neoclassicism* whose rival leaders were Sir William Chambers (1723–1796) and Robert Adam (1728–1792) (*Gazetteer* no 43). Chambers fought for a scholarly Roman style though he was much influenced by contemporary French theories (which you will study in more detail in Unit 29). Robert Adam provided an altogether more romantic classicism, based on discoveries at Pompeii and Palmyra and in Greece and Dalmatia[2], which attempted to recreate the spirit of classical architecture. Alongside, and increasingly superseding the new Neoclassicism was a strand of romanticism that produced buildings in various fanciful Chinese styles, but which is generally associated with the *gothick* style. Gothic architecture had never completely disappeared but became more fashionable towards the end of our period and is closely associated with the rise of the *picturesque*.

This brief survey of styles is intended only to give you a rough outline against which to set the buildings we shall study. I have put certain key words in italics to remind you of the rather nebulous concepts which I shall try to identify in later sections. All the architects I have named were involved in country-house building or alteration, though it is worth remembering that James Gibbs' best works were his churches (e.g. St Martin-in-the-Fields 1722–26) and his university building (the Radcliffe Library, Oxford 1737–48 and the Senate House, Cambridge 1722–30). Sir William Chambers built few country houses from scratch but was the most important government architect from the 1760s onwards (he built Somerset House 1776–96) and his book *A Treatise on Civil Architecture* (see the Course Anthology Vol 2) was particularly influential.

[2] Adam's first publication, *The Ruins of the Palace of the Emperor Diocletian at Spalato* (1764), was the splendidly illustrated result of his own explorations there in 1757.

2 The Importance of Country-House Architecture and its Development from 1715 to 1770

It doesn't make much sense to ask 'what was a country house?' without asking 'what was a country house for?'. In the eighteenth century land was still the only acceptable basis of power and the country house was both the administrative centre of each huge estate and the symbol of the prestige and extent of the owner's 'interest'.[3] The years from 1640 to 1714 had seen political turmoil and changes of dynasty which had left few of the great families unscathed. After the advent of the Hanoverians there came a stability that allowed the aristocracy to restore, enlarge or rebuild their mansions and estates. For the Whigs, now in the ascendant, the privileges of office provided ample opportunity for building. Their rivals (Tories, Catholics and supporters of the Stuarts) might find it more difficult to finance building, but it was no less important if they were to maintain their prestige. The manners, modes and buildings of the great were, of course, copied by the lesser gentry as far as they were able.

The eighteenth-century house also saw a dramatic change in the life style of its occupants and the new houses catered for the new trends. The formal pattern of Jacobean life, closely related to the medieval world and with an elaborate, almost religious ritual, was virtually gone and with it the use of medieval-style great halls and lords' chambers. In their place we find the hall as a grand entrance vestibule and the chamber transformed into a saloon.[4] These and other changes reflected a growing distance between the gentry and the lower orders, and servants' rooms were increasingly hived off into separate wings or attics. (Separate kitchens were already common and the disadvantages in terms of cold food seem not to have bothered the occupants.) The way of life of the owners was changing too. A great lord of the seventeenth century would live in considerable state and was expected to hunt well and cut a dash but need not be especially cultured. You will probably recognize Squire Western in *Tom Jones* as old-fashioned in this way; and by the middle of the eighteenth century the old ways were generally satirized as boorish and stuffy. You will see in Hogarth's *Marriage à-la-Mode* (Unit 7 plate 8) how the old-fashioned earl sits under (or at least near) a canopy such as would always have covered his chair in an earlier age.[5] However, in the eighteenth century such formality as required a permanent canopy over the lord's throne, a relic of medieval days, finally disappeared and one consequence was that the large personal following was replaced by an increasingly anonymous corps of servants (perhaps around fifty in a large household) who could appear on demand by way of separate service stairs and concealed doors.

Instead of sets of large apartments to accommodate whole households visiting for a long time we find smaller guest rooms (usually a bedroom and one or more large dressing rooms used as sitting rooms) often filling a whole separate wing. The state

[3] The term is used to describe the system of power that rested on the giving of favours and promotion in return for votes and political support; it was the key to eighteenth-century public life.

[4] The survival of state bedrooms among the eighteenth-century suites of public rooms is an interesting hangover from the medieval world. They were not regularly slept in but were a splendid excuse for show—as at Houghton Hall.

[5] A few such survived into the eighteenth century and the Duke of Norfolk for instance ate under a canopy at Norfolk House until at least 1750. Notice in the same plate the Palladian plan for the Earl's new house with which Hogarth pokes fun at the universal desire to keep up with the Jones's.

rooms were designed to suit the different pastimes—dancing, cards, reading and music—rather than being arranged as a series of increasingly private and inaccessible chambers. They were laid out *en suite*, so that one could pass in a circuit through all the rooms and return to the entrance. The private rooms of the family were kept apart, sometimes in a separate wing as at Holkham or forming a separate adjoining circuit as at Hagley (the home of the Lyttleton family to whom Fielding intended to dedicate *Tom Jones*) or Harewood (see *Gazetteer* nos 19 and 29).

Increased mobility helped to spread country house building. Better carriages and roads meant that people were readier to travel, though Sophia's journey (*Tom Jones*, Book XI chapter 2) should show you how difficult it still was. In architecture the result was a more rapid diffusion of styles and more competition.[6]

When you visit a house or study its plan always try to find out how it worked. Try to discover what each room was for, discover how the servants and the gentry gained access, and try to see how the servants' quarters relate to the rest of the house. Some knowledge of the history of the period may help you to understand the status and attitudes of the original owners (see Units 4–5).

[6] The houses and grounds were usually open to any member of polite society and the great houses were frequently crowded with visitors, so that lesser gentry were able to note and later copy grand houses they had seen. In 1776, Mrs Lybbe Powis, on her way to see Stourhead, noted that 2324 persons had visited Wilton House in the previous year.

3 Architectural Practice

It is worth looking at some of the typical personalities involved in the architecture of the period. You need not feel you have to remember details of this section but rather bear the biographical outlines in mind as typical of the sort of people involved.

Patrons

The new patrons who set the standards of taste were dilettanti—men who had studied the classics, made extensive tours of Italy and who were busy collecting pictures and ancient works of art which had to be specially housed in their new mansions. Richard Boyle (1694–1753), third Earl of Burlington, is just one of several such men, though he is outstanding in his dominance in the aesthetic field. At the age of ten he succeeded to the title and to an immense fortune, with huge estates in the East Riding and land in Piccadilly and Middlesex. He visited Italy in 1714–15 and again in 1719 making a collection of Palladio's drawings. His interest in architecture developed to a point where he himself designed several buildings (notably Chiswick House *c* 1723–29, and the Assembly Rooms at York 1731–32). He was the acknowledged leader of the Palladian School and his position as a powerful Whig aristocrat was crucial in obtaining patronage for the architects he approved of and in spreading the style.

Architects

Architects were not trained in the modern sense but the leading designers occupied a position on the fringes of noble society from whom their patrons were drawn. They needed to be sufficiently cultured to mix easily in society but they were clearly also experienced draughtsmen and able to control a small corps of workmen, plasterers, painters and carvers. I have selected four men as typical.

1 *William Kent* (*c* 1685–1748) began as an apprentice coach painter but was fortunate in finding patrons to send him to Italy in 1709 'to promote his studyes'. He acted as a buying agent for works of art and worked as a painter. He met Lord Burlington in Rome and returned with him to paint ceilings and other decorative panels. His new patron secured for him court commissions but he was not a great success. It was not until the 1730s that his work as an architect and interior designer began and here he was enormously successful designing a large number of private houses and garden monuments and also, as a member of the Board of Works and later Master Mason to the King, several important public buildings.

2 *James Gibbs* (1682–1754), a Roman Catholic (he was even a candidate for the priesthood), a Tory and a Scot, was rather suspect and found difficulty in obtaining patronage. He had trained in Rome (1703–9) under the leading Roman architect of the day and was probably better qualified than any of his contemporaries when he returned to find patronage from the Roman Catholic Earl of Mar. He kept his religious views largely hidden however, and through Tory patronage was involved in the profitable development of the Marylebone estate in London. After 1727 he gained patronage of the Whig Duke of Argyll and his success was assured. He produced many splendid buildings—houses, churches and university buildings—in a rather more dramatic and flamboyant style than contemporary Palladians.

3 *Lancelot 'Capability' Brown* (1716–1783) began work as a gardener in Northumberland at the age of sixteen. He first achieved advancement when in 1741

he was appointed head gardener to Lord Cobham at Stowe, where he worked as Kent's assistant in laying out the gardens. Over the next thirty years he was commissioned to design landscapes throughout the country. He also designed houses in the Palladian style, experimented with Gothick and had a considerable reputation as an architect. He is untypical in having trained and worked entirely in this country.

4 *Robert Adam* (1728–92) was the second son of William Adam, an established architect in Scotland. Through his father's position and his education in Edinburgh he mixed with many of the leading figures of the Scottish Enlightenment, notably Adam Smith and Hume. He did not travel until relatively late in life but spent three years (1754–58) in Italy and Dalmatia systematically studying ancient remains and renaissance architecture, a tour that cost him between £800 and £900 a year. On his return he set up in practice in London with his brothers James and William and collected a group of highly skilled craftsmen, painters and plasterers to execute his designs. The firm was enormously prolific and for thirty years he must have been the busiest architect in the country; yet the majority of his work was in alterations, additions and decoration of already existing houses. His great contribution was the recreation of Roman interior decoration.

Builder-designers and the spread of fashion

It is impossible to draw a firm line between architects and builders but the wide spread of the fashions of Georgian buildings is due to many others apart from the great designers. Most of the better known architects published illustrated books of their work or theories of architecture but there were also a number who published pattern books that provided even the humblest craftsmen with designs to work from (fig 1). The books were quite widely bought by the gentry and one has to envisage the lesser patrons perhaps borrowing books from noble friends to show their local carpenter or builder what was needed.

Batty Langley (see the Course Anthology Vol 2 and radio programme 6) was undoubtedly the most prolific of these men, producing books on gardening, geometry, carpentry, the five orders, gothick architecture and the like, replete with patterns of all sorts. Also typical was William Halfpenny who worked mostly in the west country but published widely; Abraham Swan is another who produced books such as *The Builders Treasury of Staircases* (1745) and *One Hundred and Fifty New Designs for Chimney Pieces* (1758).

4 Theories and Styles

The rise of Palladianism

Palladian was the most fashionable style from about 1715 to 1750 and was based on a rigid theory of proportion (see p. 22). It was named after the Italian architect Andrea Palladio (1508–80) who wrote a treatise called the *Four Books of Architecture* in 1570. This presented the ideas of the Roman Vitruvius who wrote a book on architecture during the reign of Augustus (31 BC–14 AD). Palladio studied Roman remains but also adapted them to build churches, palaces and country estates in and around Venice. His ideas were influential in Europe and in particular were taken up by Inigo Jones (1573–1652) in this country. Palladio's book was widely translated from 1663, but the early English versions were only of part of the book, translated at second-hand via the French and poorly illustrated. The first accurate, well-illustrated translation from Italian to English was made by Nicholas Du Bois and Giacomo Leoni and published in 1716. Read the following extracts from the introduction. What are the main points that Leoni makes?

> Everyone may rest satisfy'd that the fine new Translations publish'd in this Volume, and join'd to the Italian Original, are very faithful, and that I have left nothing unattempted to make them as perfect as could be wish'd . . . All good Judges must need own that we wanted to Work of this Nature; and there is no doubt, but it will prove very useful, as much to Architects and Workmen, as to those who design to build for themselves; since it contains the necessary Rules for raising the plainest Buildings, as well as the most adorn'd. Everybody cannot build Palaces, nor enrich their Houses with Columns, Pilasters and so many other Ornaments of Architecture, which require great charges. But since there are no Houses, tho never so small, without doors and windows, and some of the other parts, first invented by necessity, and then adorn'd that they might be more graceful, it is not more chargeable to make them according to their just proportions, by following the directions of some intelligent Person than to leave them to the management and discretion of the workmen, who generally mind nothing but what is profitable to them. . .
>
> Hence it is that we see so many bungl'd Houses and so oddly contriv'd, that they seem to have been made only to be admir'd by ignorant Men, and to raise the laughter of those who are sensible of such imperfections. Most of them are like Birdcages, by reason of the largeness and too great number of windows; or like prisons, because of the Darkness of the rooms, passages and stairs. Some want the most essential part, I mean the Entablature or Cornice; and tho it be the best fence against the injuries of the Weather, it is left out to save charges. In some other Houses the rooms are so small and strait, that one knows not where to place the most necessary furniture. Others, through the oddness of some new and insignificant ornaments, seem to exceed the wildest Gothick. It were an endless thing to enumerate all the absurdities, which many of our Builders introduce every day into their way of building. . .
>
> Many Persons, even among the most illustrious Nobility, begin to relish Architecture. They take delight in learning its most beautiful proportions; and by comparing the buildings of eminent and experienc'd Architects with those that have been rais'd by unskilful Men, they easily perceive what a vast difference there is between the noble productions of the former, and the extravagant performances of the latter.

Discussion

He states the need for a widely available book on architectural theory, and claims that the Palladian system provides a set of universal rules. By pushing his book as the intellectual cornerstone of the only sound architecture Leoni was making a bid to become the chief promoter and arbiter of the new style. Actually he was too much of an individualist and though his illustrations are fine he saw no objection to altering some of Palladio's designs to make them more 'modern'. The book was a sumptuous production which suggests that it was aimed at connoisseurs of the highest rank.

Leoni had accurately judged the time to be ripe for a new style but his book was anticipated by Colen Campbell's *Vitruvius Britannicus* in 1715 to which Leoni refers. This was an equally lavish production that consisted of a collection of English buildings and designs by Campbell together with his critical comments and a polemical preface. Read the following extract:

> The general esteem that Travellers have for Things that are Foreign, is in nothing more conspicuous than with Regard to Building. We travel, for the most part, at an Age more apt to be imposed upon by the Ignorance or Partiality of others, than to judge truly the Merit of Things by the Strength of Reason. It's owing to this Mistake in Education, that so many of the British Quality have so mean an Opinion of what is performed in our own Country, tho', perhaps, in most we equal, and in some Things we surpass, our Neighbours.
>
> We must, In Justice, acknowledge very great Obligations to those Explorers of Architecture, which the Fifteenth and Sixteenth Centurys produced in Italy. But above all, the great Palladio, who has exceeded all that were gone before him, and surpassed his Contemporaries, whose ingenious Labours will eclipse many, and rival most of the Ancients. And indeed, this excellent Architect seems to have arrived to a Ne plus ultra[7] of his Art.
>
> Colen Campbell *Vitruvius Britannicus* (1715)

Discussion

Campbell, like Leoni, sees the new Classical architecture as the only true style and declares Palladio as its chief prophet. He goes on to praise Inigo Jones and others, as evidence that British architecture should not be rated so low.

This element of national pride is important in the adoption of Palladianism. Read these extracts from Lord Shaftesbury's *Letter Concerning Design* (written in 1712, published in 1732):

> This in the mean time I can, with some assurance, say to your Lordship in a kind of spirit of prophecy, from what I have observ'd of the rising Genius of our Nation, That the Figure we are like to make abroad, and the Increase of Knowledge, Industry and Sense at home, will render *united* BRITAIN the principal Seat of the Arts . . .
>
> As for ARCHITECTURE, 'tis no wonder if so many noble Designs of this kind have miscarry'd amongst us: since the Genius of our Nation has hitherto been so little turn'd this way, that thro' several Reigns we have patiently seen the noblest publick Buildings perish (if I may say so) under the Hand of one single Court-Architect[8]; who, if he had been able to profit by experience, have prov'd the greatest Master in the World. But I question whether our Patience is like to hold much longer. The Devastation so long committed in this kind, has made us begin to grow rude and clamorous at the hearing of a new Palace spoilt, or a new Design committed to some rash or impotent Pretender.

[7] The Latin tag means 'The highest possible pinnacle of achievement'.

[8] He clearly means Sir Christopher Wren (1632–1723)

Discussion

Shaftesbury clearly despised the baroque work of Wren and claimed the time was ripe for change. The new style was finally launched by Richard Boyle third Earl of Burlington (see p. 10) whose patronage made the new buildings possible.

Exercise

How did Palladianism come to Britain and what were the main elements in its ancestry?

Discussion

Palladianism appeared in Britain first in the works of Inigo Jones, but the first conscious imitation, a revival of both Palladio's style and that of Inigo Jones, was launched around 1715 by the books published by Giacomo Leoni and Colen Campbell and by the interest of Lord Burlington. Palladio's own work was a revival of Roman architecture as described by Vitruvius. British Palladianism is thus a revival of a revival, with the added influence of subsidiary strains from Inigo Jones. After Campbell and Leoni there were a number of further publications many by less able and talented men such as Edward Hoppus (see fig 8). These helped to spread the gospel widely.

The reaction against Palladianism

There had always been a problem that Palladio's architecture was adapted for north Italian villas of the sixteenth century and was unsuitable in planning for either the British climate or eighteenth-century society. So strong, though, was Lord Burlington's influence as an arbiter of taste (and as a source of influence in obtaining commissions) that it was impossible for builders to ignore Palladian doctrine.

Robert Adam was the first to break free with a new style based on wide research among the ruins of Rome. He learned that Roman architecture provided far more variety than was suggested by the theories of Palladio and the resulting freedom made the task of adapting classical ideas to the needs of the eighteenth-century British nobility substantially easier. The general layout of the country houses, with suites of grand rooms and wings for family, visitors and servants, did not change greatly. The shape and decoration of the rooms did, with Roman motifs from the whole of the imperial period gathered and reassembled into increasingly homogeneous schemes (compare fig 35 and plate 1). After the mid 1750s Palladianism in England was gradually superseded by Neoclassicism. The term 'neoclassical' is difficult to define, but with reference to eighteenth-century architecture is best thought of as a synthesis of the 'intellectual' classicism of the previous generation with the romantic naturalism previously confined to landscape architecture[9]. In the eighteenth century at least Neoclassicism was *not* simply strict copying from ancient Greek or Roman models. This might seem odd, for the period was one of increasing scholarship and developing archaeology. One of the most influential books was Stuart and Revett's *Antiquities of Athens* (vol 1 1762). Read the extract from the introduction to their work in the Course Anthology Vol 2.

They stress the accuracy and scientific approach of their work and claim the primacy of Greek as opposed to Roman sources. Though their work was widely admired and was important in the development of rational scholarship it had little direct influence on British architecture. In Italy however the rediscovery of Greece led to a passionate championship of Rome by G. B. Piranesi (1720–1778). His writings and etchings influenced romantic neoclassicism and the exciting excavations

[9] See C. Hussey *English Country Houses, Mid Georgian 1760–1860* (1955), Country Life.

at Pompeii (from around 1750 on) provided plenty of detailed inspiration. The romance of these ruins fitted nicely with the philosophical current of Hume's *Essay on Taste* (1767) and Burke's *Enquiry on the Sublime and Beautiful* (1757) which stressed intuitive feeling rather than intellect.

Alternatives to the classical

Besides the great mass of classical work there were a number of Gothick[10] buildings (figs 29–30). This style, which became very popular at the end of the eighteenth century, received its first major impetus when Horace Walpole set about gothicizing his villa Strawberry Hill at Twickenham in 1750 (see television programme 3). However his was not a completely new discovery for the old gothic traditions had never completely died out.

It has to be remembered, first of all, that in the eighteenth century there was more original medieval work about than now, in the shape of untouched village churches

Figure 2 Claydon House, Buckinghamshire, the Chinese Room, 1769, Lightfoot. Photograph Edwin Smith.

[10] By convention, eighteenth-century gothic revival is referred to as 'Gothick' while 'gothic' is used to denote medieval gothic building.

and monastic remains often converted as dwellings. Gothic details had an immediate appeal and William Kent (see p. 10) began to use them as a new range of patterns in garden buildings from about 1740 on. There was an attempt to rationalize the study of gothic in Batty Langley's *Gothic Architecture Restored and Improved* (1742) (see radio programme 6), but the chief attraction was the prettiness and picturesque quality of the ogee arches and decorative carving which afforded a welcome alternative to the severe formality of classical buildings.

Further variety was provided by the various exotic styles. The opening up of Canton after 1700 led to an interest in Chinese designs (although there was little attempt to distinguish between Chinese, Japanese and even Hindu styles). Here was a whole new set of patterns and shapes that could be used for garden buildings or interior decoration (fig 2). They generally have a light and frivolous delicacy that matches the Continental rococo style. Rococo is the term used to describe the delicate and usually assymetrical decoration, often based on the shell motif that was particularly popular in France and Germany in the first half of the eighteenth century. Continental rococo continued to make use of classical motifs, often wilfully distorted.

These new styles can be seen as shifting the emphasis from the intellectual to the romantic and were influential in two areas.

1 In the planning of parks and gardens (see also pp. 48–52). From very early on, the design of landscape provided a romantic contrast to the severe Palladian houses. Charles Bridgeman (*d* 1738), Royal Gardener to George II, began a development that was to break down the barrier between the formal garden (see fig 36) and the open country by use of the ha-ha, or sunken fence. He was responsible for the gardens at Hampton Court, Hyde Park and Marble Hill among others. The best known of his successors was Lancelot 'Capability' Brown (1716–1783), whose enormous popularity is shown in the many parks he had a hand in shaping (figs 3 and 37) (though few survive intact) and his influence soon spread down the social scale to touch the aspirations of the rising middle classes.

> ten guineas if I remember right is the price of a single call, with or without the advantage of his direction, to make a Lawn and piece of Water here—Cut down that wood and plant it there, level that rising ground and raise yonder valley &c. &c.
>
> J. Wedgwood, letter to T. Bentley, 15 September 1766; Wedgwood *Letters to Bentley* vol I, privately published 1903

Wedgwood, the self-made pottery magnate, provides an apt summary of Capability Brown's recipe of carefully sited artificial serpentine lakes, green meadows and woodland clumps. The aim of combining art with nature was more subtly described by Pope:

> Consult the genius of the place in all:
> That tells the Waters or to rise, or fall,
> Or helps th'ambitious Hill the heavens to scale,
> Or scoops in circling theatres the Vale,
> Calls in the Country, catches opening glades,
> Joins willing woods, and varies shades from shades,
> Now breaks, or now directs, th'intending Lines;
> Paints as you plant, and, as you work, designs.
> Still follow Sense, of ev'ry Art the Soul.
> Parts answering parts shall slide into a whole,
> Spontaneous beauties all around advance.
> Start ev'n from Difficulty, strike from Chance;
> Nature shall join you, Time shall make it grow
> A Work to wonder at—perhaps a STOW.
>
> Alexander Pope *Epistle to Lord Burlington*, 54–70

Figure 3 Petworth, Sussex, landscape, *c* 1753, 'Capability' Brown. Photograph Edwin Smith.

It was at Stowe near Buckingham (see *Gazetteer* no 9) that Bridgeman, Kent and Brown created for Lord Cobham one of the most splendid and extravagant garden layouts of the day. The importance of the idyllic setting is also made clear in Fielding's description of Allworthy's park[11] (*Tom Jones*, pp. 58–9).

2 In interior decoration. The spread of scholarship and the publication of illustrated books enormously increased the range of sources from which decorators could draw. The taste for the antique was as much romantic as intellectual and the pillaging of Roman sculpture and Greek vases from Italy by visiting milords was supplemented by antique-inspired reproductions. These treasures were displayed in their houses and suitable decoration devised to show them off. The enormously rich variety offered by designers such as Robert Adam was the product of sensitive imagination drawing on a wealth of studies of Roman originals systematically collected during his four-year stay in Italy (and supported by a team of highly skilled craftsmen). To have a house decorated in this way was to be up-to-date, but the essential quality of Adam's work is its immediate visual appeal rather than any underlying logic (although there was that too). Robert Adam had a keen eye for the visually appealing and so his combinations of motifs from a wide range of sources are usually easy on the eye, full of variety and movement but always a unity.

[11] It is curious that there is no mention of farming but only of the pleasure grounds. There would surely have been farms to support 'one of the largest estates in the country' (p. 53) but it is generally accepted that Allworthy is based on the character of Ralph Allen of Bath (see television programme 2), whose estate at Prior Park in Somerset was unique at the time in being supported on the proceeds of his commercial undertakings.

5 The Language of Architecture

There are about a million Georgian houses still surviving in this country[12]. What is it about these buildings that provides such a lasting joy and makes them such a pleasure to look at?

First, I think, the classical styles impose a logical order on the whole composition so that though these houses may be dull, they seldom look uncomfortable. Second,

Figure 4 Clyffe Hall, Market Lavington, Wiltshire, 1737. Photograph National Monuments Record, London.

Figure 5 Peckover House, Wisbech, Cambridgeshire, 1732. Photograph The National Trust.

[12] John Woodforde *Georgian Houses for All* (1978), Routledge and Kegan Paul. The figure is for the whole Georgian period from 1700–1830, i.e. including Queen Anne and the Regency.

Figure 6 Stourhead House, Wiltshire, 1721–4, Colen Campbell, east elevation. From Colen Campbell *Vitruvius Britannicus*, vol III (1725), plate 42. Photograph from 1967 reprint by Benjamin Blom Books.

the hallmark of Georgian building is proportion. All the parts, doors, windows, fireplaces, plan and elevation are related to each other according to a system of mathematical proportion so that each house is felt as a unity.

Exercise

Look at the three houses illustrated (figs 4–6). How are the classical elements (columns etc.) used? How do windows relate to wall space and how are the different floors suggested by the design of the facade?

Discussion

All three houses are symmetrically composed and all make use of columns, pilasters, pediments, etc. but in different ways. In the small mansion (fig 4) the whole design is controlled by the pilasters. Notice the heavy cornice and the way the corners are stressed by the angle quoins and see how the great Corinthian pilasters relate to the small Ionic columns of the doorway. This house retains some old-fashioned features and the parts do not relate as well as those of Stourhead House (fig 6). The roof is not concealed by a parapet; the pediment and pilasters are the main feature, but clearly dramatic rather than structural—a baroque touch. The central part is large, but the side bays seem rather cramped and there are no simple underlying geometrical relations. There are elements of the baroque (for definition, see *Gazetteer*) in this facade, but the basic classical unity is clear.

Peckover House (fig 5) is plainer but there is the same easy relationship between the parts. Again the whole facade is united by the cornice and the parapet hides the roof. At the corners are pilasters which appear to support the cornice. See how the three floors are marked off by a projecting strip and how the windows with the panel of contrasting brick below seem to stand on those strips. The actual door is much lower than the ground floor windows but is given prominence by a frame that roughly doubles its height. See too how the windows of each floor are smaller than those below but retain the pattern of three by four panes.

Stourhead (fig 6) is altogether grander and larger but with an even clearer unity. This was one of the first great Palladian mansions to be built. Here there is an actual temple front as a portico rising the whole height of the building its pediment echoed in smaller pediments over the windows of the main floor. The whole design is raised on a podium, which housed kitchen and servants, equal in height to the cornice and balustrade, but made to look more solid by its rusticated stone work while the balustrade being pierced is lighter. The statues and urns give a lift to the plain rectangle that without its base course is almost exactly twice as long as it is high. The urns also stress the corners that here have no quoins or pilasters. Because the temple front rises the whole height of the building, the architect has not divided the floors by an intermediate cornice but the windows make the different functions of the rooms clear. The upper floors have square windows while those of the 'parade' rooms are twice as high as they are wide.

One could go on listing subtle relationships but I think the principle is clear enough. This sort of structured composition was made easier in plans and facades because there was a clearly recognized 'language' of architectural forms and ornamental motifs each with established proportions. The underlying pattern is perceived by the eye and appears easy and attractive and, as in all classical designs, a basic symmetry was crucial.

The parts of a building

Like any art architecture has a detailed technical language of its own which is essential in enabling builders to interpret plans and instructions. You will not need to master more than the few basic terms which are illustrated below (fig 7).

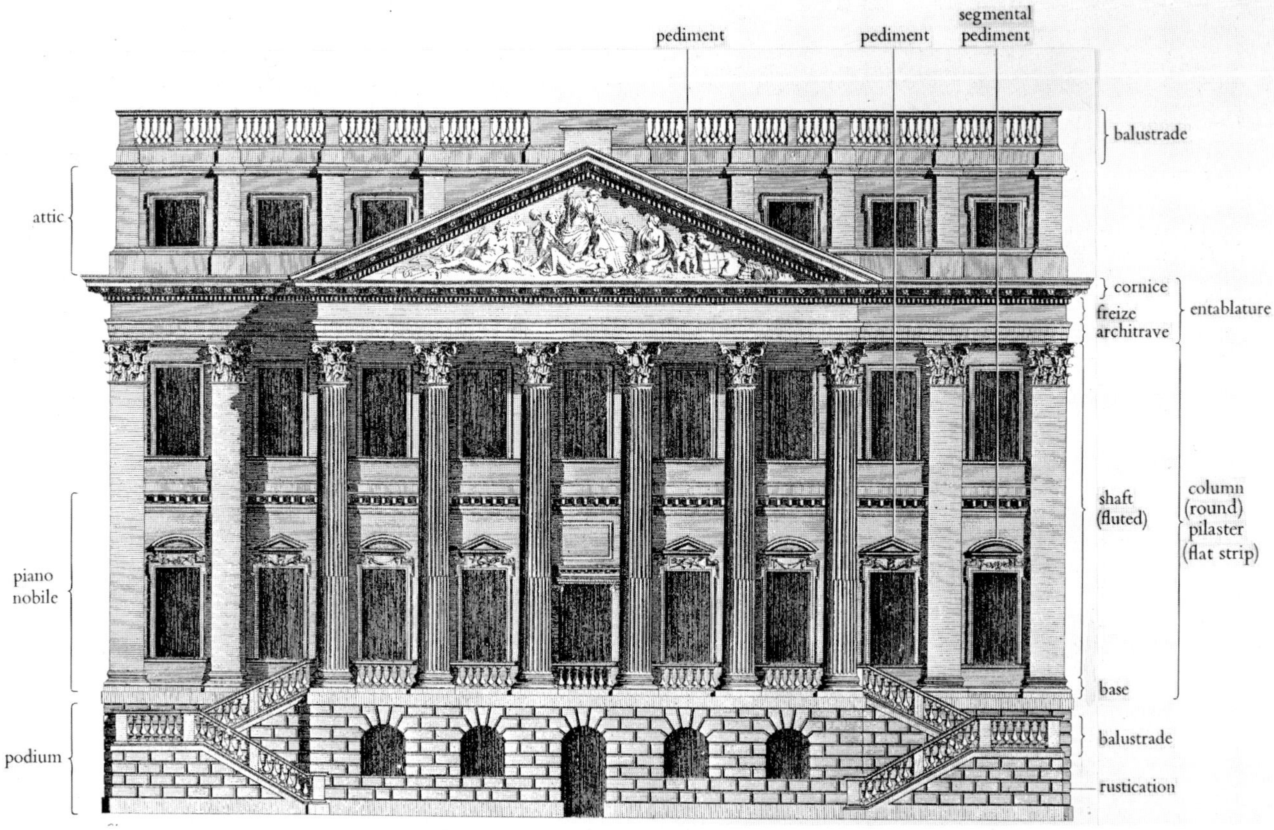

Figure 7 Mansion House, London, 1739–53, George Dance, elevation. From Woolfe and Gandon *Vitruvius Britannicus*, vol IV (1767), plate 42. Photograph from 1967 reprint by Benjamin Blom Books.

The five orders

The design of Palladian and neoclassical buildings is based on the five 'orders' of ancient architecture: Tuscan, Doric, Ionic, Corinthian and Composite. Make sure that you can identify the different patterns and the different parts from the plates below.

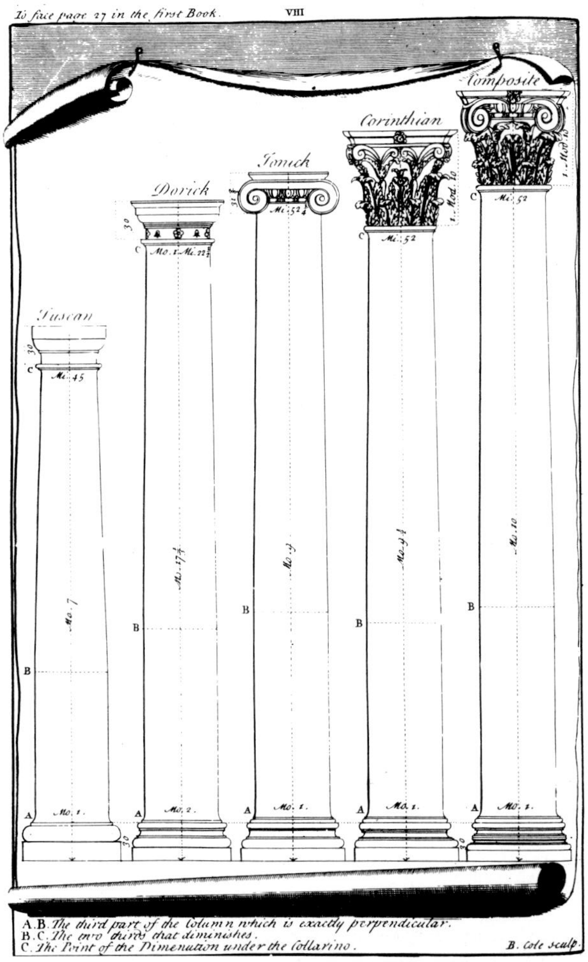

Figure 8 (left) 1 Tuscan, 2 Doric, 3 Ionic, 4 Corinthian, 5 Composite. From Palladio *Four Books on Architecture* edited by Hoppus (1733), plate VIII. Photograph Cambridge University Library, reproduced by permission of the Syndics.

Figure 9 (bottom left) Detail of the Doric order, showing the ornament on the entablature and underside of the cornice. From Palladio *Four Books on Architecture*, edited by Hoppus (1733), plate XI. Photograph Cambridge University Library, reproduced by permission of the Syndics.

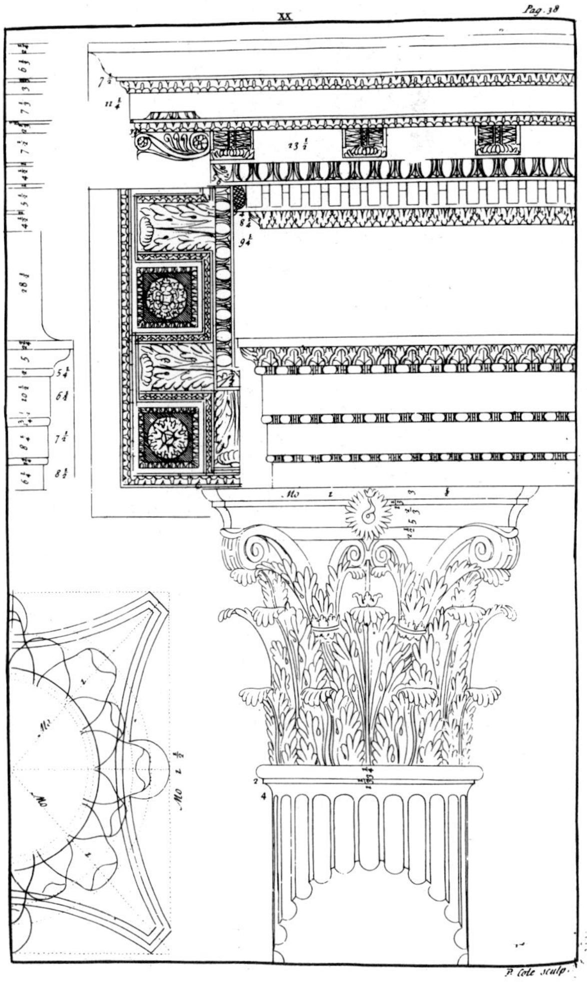

Figure 10 (bottom right) Detail of the Corinthian order, showing the ornament on the entablature and underside of the cornice. From Palladio *Four Books on Architecture*, edited by Hoppus (1733), plate XX. Photograph Cambridge University Library, reproduced by permission of the Syndics.

The difference in shape is obvious, but don't forget that the order in fact means the Pedestal, (if there was one), the Column (base, shaft and capital) and the Entablature (architrave frieze and cornice). These columns could be used as straight supports or adapted for use with arches (but see Laugier, Course Anthology Vol 2 and radio programme 6). The actual disposition of the ornament and shape of the flutes was carefully controlled (see figs 9 and 10) so that the logic of their relationship was clearly defined. Check the position of the carved members in figures 14–35. Above all, though, the columns were distinguished by their different proportions. These were governed by a basic module, the base diameter of the column (or half the diameter in Doric), which was divided into 60 'minutes' and from which all the other dimensions were calculated (see figs 9 and 10). See what a different impression is given by altering the spacing of the columns (fig 11). You can see that a careful geometry underlay the use of these orders.

The Palladian system

Palladio had a good deal to say about the five orders and set out detailed rules (see table), but reckoned that the Corinthian 'is more elegant and strikes the eye more agreeably than any other'.

Palladio's recipe of proportions for the five orders
(Measurements in modules)

		Tuscan	**Doric***	**Ionic**	**Corinthian**	**Composite**
	base	$\frac{1}{2}$	$\frac{1}{2}$	$\frac{1}{2}$	$\frac{1}{2}$	$\frac{1}{2}$
	projection of base	$\frac{1}{6}$	$\frac{1}{6}$	—	—	—
	column	7	$7\frac{1}{2}$–8	9	$9\frac{1}{2}$	10
	capital	$\frac{1}{2}$	1	$31\frac{2}{3}$ minutes	$1\frac{1}{6}$	$1\frac{1}{6}$
entablatures	architrave	height = breadth	$\frac{1}{2}$	36 minutes } $\frac{1}{5}$ column	36 minutes }	2
entablatures	frieze		$\frac{3}{4}$	27 minutes } $\frac{1}{5}$ column	27 minutes }	2
entablatures	cornice		$\frac{7}{12}$	45 minutes } $\frac{1}{5}$ column	45 minutes }	2
	cornice projection	—	$\frac{1}{3}$	—	—	—
	inter-columniation	3 or more	3	$2\frac{1}{4}$	2	$1\frac{1}{2}$

*For convenience these figures are converted to the standard module of the whole base diameter.

In Palladian houses all the rest of the planning was also governed by proportion carefully geared to the human scale. For instance Palladio ruled that stairs should be light, large and easy to ascend; they should not be less than four feet wide; risers should be not more than six inches and not less than four inches; treads should be from one foot to one foot six inches and there should be an odd number of stairs so that if you started to climb with the right foot you would end with the right foot. Windows should be not more than $\frac{1}{4}$ or less than $\frac{1}{6}$ of the breadth of the room wide and their height should be $2\frac{1}{6}$ times their width. All those on one storey should be of the same height.

For rooms he specified seven beautiful proportions: round (this shape was generally rejected by British Palladians), square, with the long side equal to the diagonal of a square formed on the short side, $1 \times 1\frac{1}{3}$, $1 \times 1\frac{1}{2}$, $1 \times 1\frac{2}{3}$, and 1×2. Their altitude was to be determined by their dimensions.

Finally the hall should be on the central axis of the house with the smaller rooms arranged symmetrically on either side. Of course his rules could not be followed precisely, after all they were designed for Italian buildings. However, the principles were absorbed and approximations to his figures were common. (Bear this in mind when you are looking at the Case Studies.) Just consider for instance the problems his instructions would cause in designing a house with both large and small rooms on the same floor. Some system of proportional relationship of the measurements was, however, *de rigueur* in Palladian buildings. (See fig 6 and the Course Anthology Vol 2 Plates 1–5.)

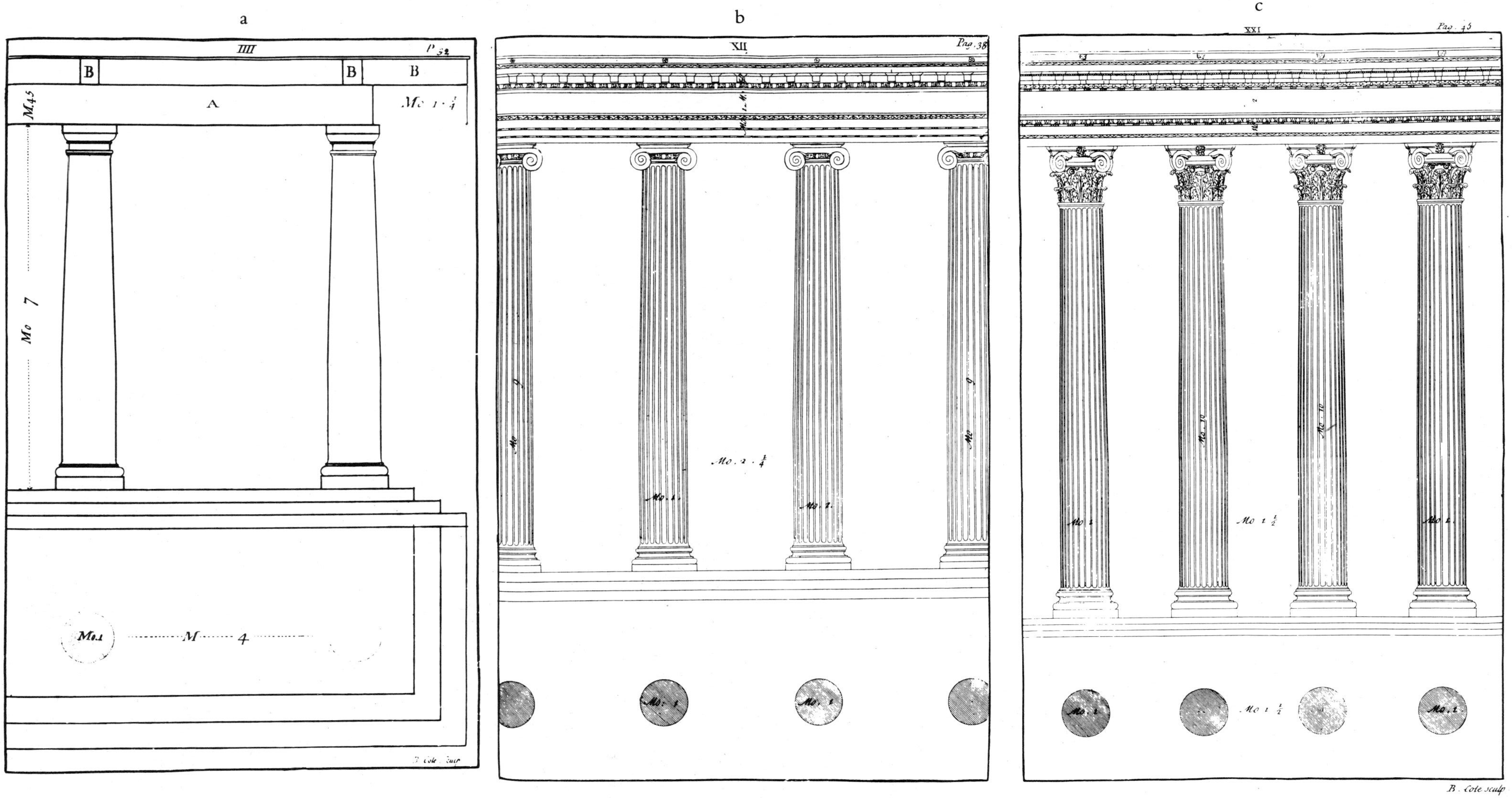

Figure 11 The spacing of columns: a four diameters apart, b two and a quarter diameters, c one and a half diameters. From Palladio *Four Books on Architecture*, edited by Hoppus (1733), plates IV, XII and XXI. Photograph Cambridge University Library Board, reproduced by permission of the Syndics.

Neoclassical ornament

The ornamental elements of classical architecture were an easily recognizable vocabulary of basic forms. Don't feel you need to remember all the names but check them on figure 12 and look for examples in the Case Studies and in any houses you visit. There were of course other motifs such as the rose often found in Ionic cornices and the ox skull of some Doric friezes (fig 9).[13] Then there are gryphons and grotesque masks, putti and vases, and the sunken coffer for ceilings, shells for niches and of course the fan shape. You can find variations of many of these in this design for a ceiling at Kenwood by Robert Adam (fig 13).

Robert Adam was the undoubted master of this sort of decoration chiefly because of the huge stock of reference drawings made during his visits to Italy. However it was not merely in the vocabulary that he was a master. His great skill lay also in devising a whole decorative scheme that formed a progression of varied and interesting shapes in place of the plain rectangles of the Palladian style. These he was able to decorate down to the last detail with his elegant and highly sophisticated designs.

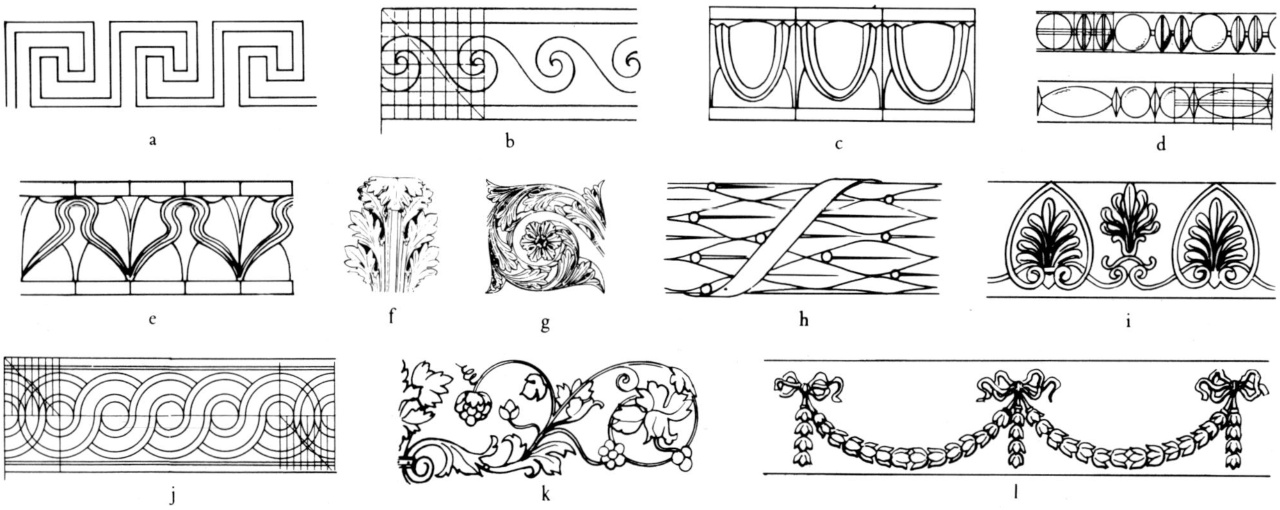

Figure 12 Classical ornamental motifs: a meander, b running wave, c egg and dart, d bead and reel, e leaf and tongue, f acanthus, g acanthus scroll, h laurel, i palmette and honeysuckle, j guilloche (or twisted strand), k vine, l swag.

[13] This was supposedly derived from the skulls of sacrificial victims which, it was imagined, were hung outside the temples of the Romans.

Figure 13 Design for the ceiling of the library, Kenwood, 1767, Robert Adam. Photograph Sir John Soane's Museum, reproduced by courtesy of the Trustees.

Case Studies

In the Case Studies I want you to concentrate on the plates, figures and plans and try to find in them features mentioned in the earlier sections. In each case be sure that you can identify the orders used and the decorative elements. Pay particular attention too to differences between the designs and the actual buildings and the ways in which the different parts echo each other.

1 Marble Hill House, Twickenham

Our first case study is a small Palladian villa built for Henrietta Howard Countess of Suffolk to the designs of Henry Herbert ninth Earl of Pembroke and the master carpenter Roger Morris. This house, relatively small[14] and properly called a villa, does not have an estate such as those at Holkham and Kedleston. Nevertheless it was very lavishly decorated (the Countess was George II's mistress—he was then Prince of Wales—and he contributed £12,000 to the cost). The basic design was influential on many later houses and was itself based on Palladio's projected Palazzo Capra in Vicenza.

Exercise

Look carefully at figs 14–16 and then try to analyse the facade and the plan. How many Palladian elements can you find here? (See p. 22.)

Figure 14 Marble Hill House, Twickenham, north or entrance facade. Photograph GLC Photographic Unit.

[14] It had an extra wing in the shape of a small building to the east that housed the Countess's china collection.

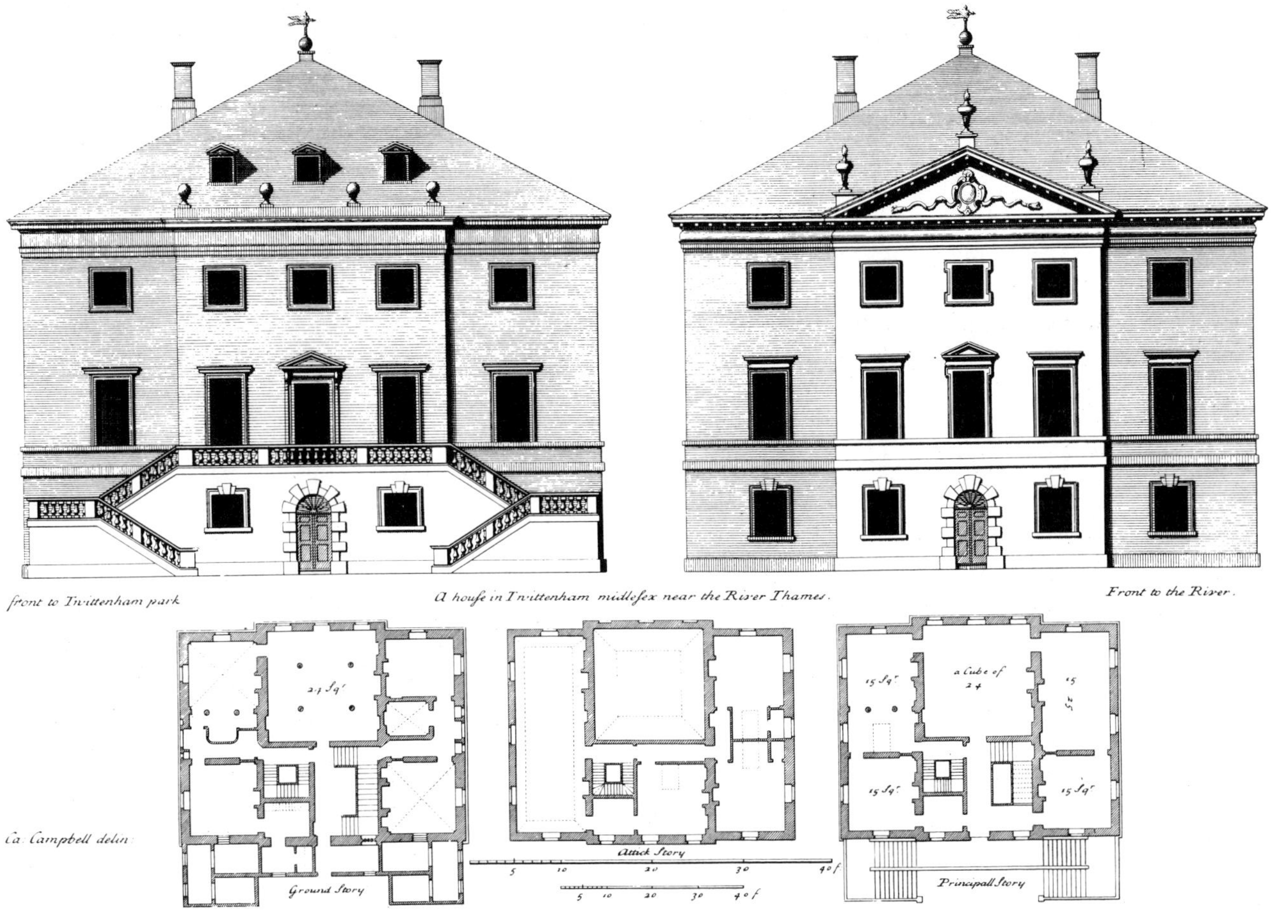

Figure 15 Marble Hill House, Twickenham, elevations and plans. From Colen Campbell *Vitruvius Britannicus*, vol III (1725), plate 93. Photograph from 1967 reprint by Benjamin Blom Books.

Figure 16 Marble Hill House, Twickenham, the Great Room. Photograph GLC Photographic Unit.

Discussion

The parts of the facade are symmetrically disposed, clearly differentiated and yet relate to each other. The basement is about half the height of the other two storeys. The upper windows are square, the main ones twice as high (and stressed by short sections of cornice), and the basement ones one and a half times as high. You can discover other relationships for yourself. All the windows on each floor are the same height with the central openings stressed. The centrepiece is a temple pattern with Ionic pilasters and the basement is rusticated to look more solid. The entrance is relatively insignificant. Notice the Palladian touch of vistas right through the house. The main rooms are on the piano nobile.[15] Notice the use of the square; and at 15 feet $\times$ 25 feet the long rooms are exactly $1 \times 1\frac{2}{3}$. In the cube room the windows at three feet wide are precisely $\frac{1}{6}$ of the breadth of the room. Finally notice how the grand stairs do not rise beyond the main floor—Lady Suffolk's bedchamber was there and the upper floor was for private use; servants were crammed into an attic in the roof.

The house is a fine example of Palladian design. Its proportions are beautiful but this was very much a luxury house, built on the proceeds of a royal liaison and when the Prince of Wales came to the throne in 1727 Swift maliciously wrote:

> My house was built but for a show
> My lady's empy pockets know
> And now she will not have a shilling
> To raise the stairs, or build the ceiling
>
> Pastoral Dialogue between Richmond Lodge and Marble Hill, 1727

2 Holkham Hall, Norfolk

This house is often regarded as the finest Palladian mansion in the country. It was built between 1734 and 1760 (fully habitable by about 1742) for Thomas Coke, Lord Leicester, as the centrepiece of a brand new farming estate. The architect for the interior was William Kent, but the original plan suggests the influence of Lord Burlington himself and we know that Lord Leicester for thirty years 'co-operated in the choice of every member and helped to bring it to perfection before it was given to the workmen to execute'. The work was supervised by Matthew Brettingham of Norwich. Look at figs 17 to 19 and consider how far they show the Palladian style.

Discussion

There are lots of points to raise; you may have spotted more than I have. Each block is clearly differentiated and they relate in proportion to each other. Though the building is actually of brick the basement is rusticated like heavy stonework. The centre of the South Front has a deep portico like a temple front. The disposition of the windows, their height and different patterns are all Palladian as is the relation of window space to solid wall. The whole is immensely solid and severe almost in contrast to the rich interior.

[15] The ground floor contained the dining room and breakfast room.

Figure 17 Holkham Hall, Norfolk, central part of south front. Photograph National Monuments Record, London.

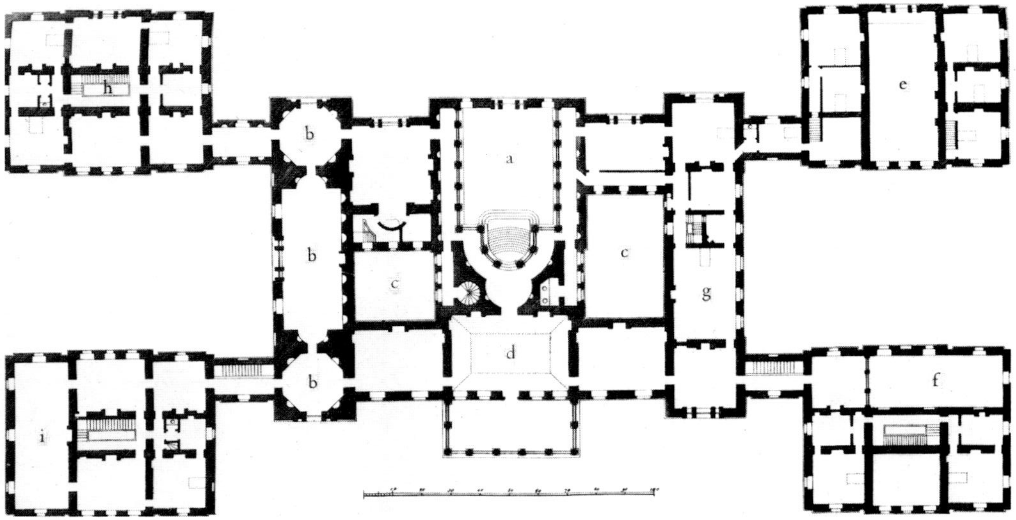

Figure 18 Holkham Hall, Norfolk, plan. a Marble Hall, b sculpture gallery, c court, d saloon, e kitchen, f chapel, g state bedroom, h visitor's wing, i library and private wing.

Figure 19 Holkham Hall, Norfolk, elevation of north facade. From Woolf and Gandon *Vitruvius Britannicus*, vol V (1771), plates 66 and 67. Photograph from 1967 reprint by Benjamin Blom Books.

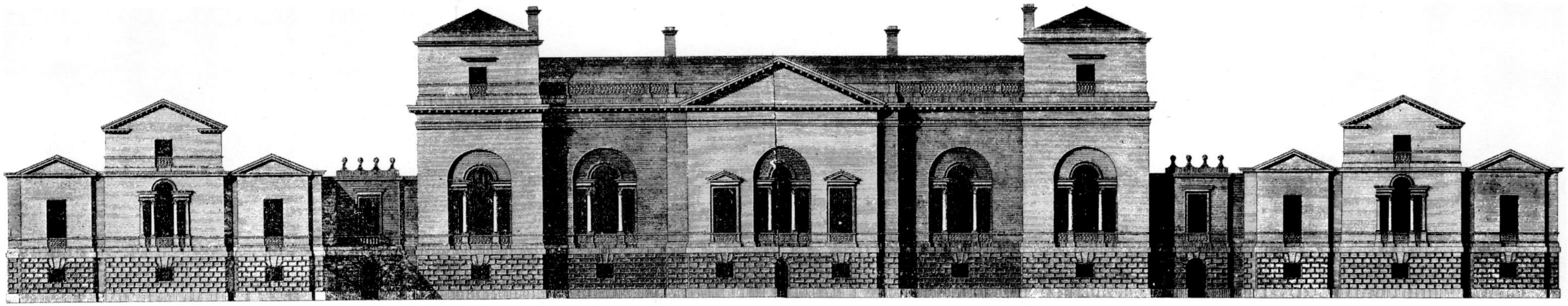

The most exciting space inside the house is the hall. Look carefully at the plan and figs 20 and 21 and consider what makes the room interesting.

Discussion

The columns exactly match the height of those on the south front and the materials and decoration are rich in the extreme. The space is very complex with the galleries, the apse and the stairs (linking a basement entry with the piano nobile was always difficult); but there is an underlying simplicity. Discounting the apse but including the galleries the space is very nearly a cube. This ambiguity of space is tantalizing but firmly based in Palladian rationality.

Figure 20 Holkham Hall, Norfolk, the Marble Hall. Photograph National Monuments Record, London.

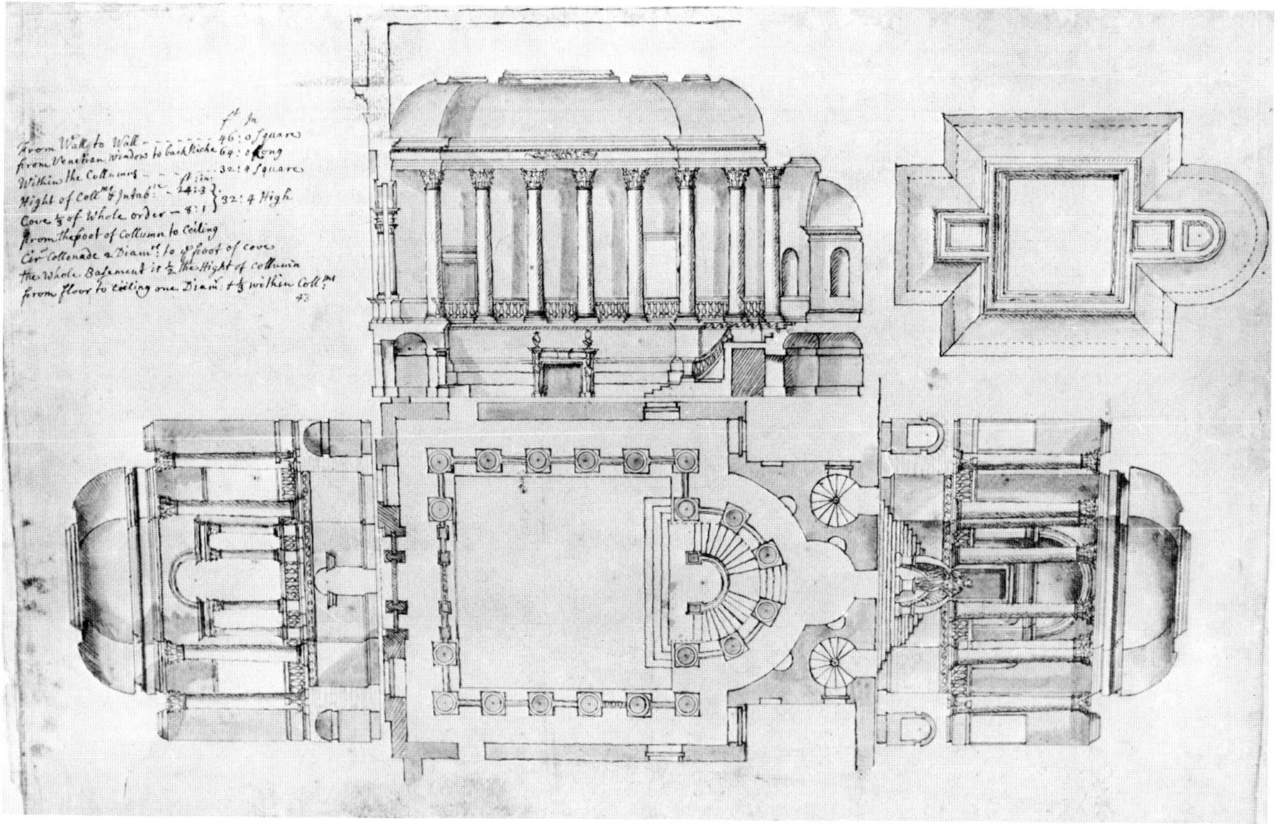

Figure 21 Holkham Hall, Norfolk, design for the Marble Hall. Lord Leicester Collection, Holkham. Photograph Courtauld Institute of Art, London © G. Higgott, reproduced by courtesy of Viscount Coke.

Figure 22 Holkham Hall, Norfolk, Statue Gallery (compare fig 35). Photograph National Monuments Record, London.

3 Kedleston Hall, Derbyshire

Kedleston Hall was one of Robert Adam's first major commissions (Harewood House was another). He was first called in in 1758, the year in which he returned from Rome, to advise on garden monuments. He soon ousted James 'Athenian' Stuart as consultant on interior decoration and after 1760 took over control of the house from James Paine and Matthew Brettingham, two firm Palladians. He adapted their designs as far as possible to his new ideas and the south front shows the new neoclassical style which superseded Palladianism. The interior, though not typical of Adam's mature style, is a considerable advance on houses such as Holkham.

Look at figs 23 to 27 and plate 2 and compare them with the illustrations of Holkham. What are the chief differences?

Figure 23 Kedleston Hall, Derbyshire, south front. Photograph Country Life, London.

Figure 24 Kedleston Hall, Derbyshire, Robert Adam's design for the south front, showing the wings that were never built. Woolfe and Gandon *Vitruvius Britannicus*, vol IV (1767), plates 49 and 50. Photograph from 1967 reprint by Benjamin Blom Books.

Figure 25 Kedleston Hall, Derbyshire, a James Paine's plan, b the plan as modified by Robert Adam. Redrawn from C. C. Hussey *English Country Houses: Mid Georgian 1760–1800* (1955), Country Life, p. 71.

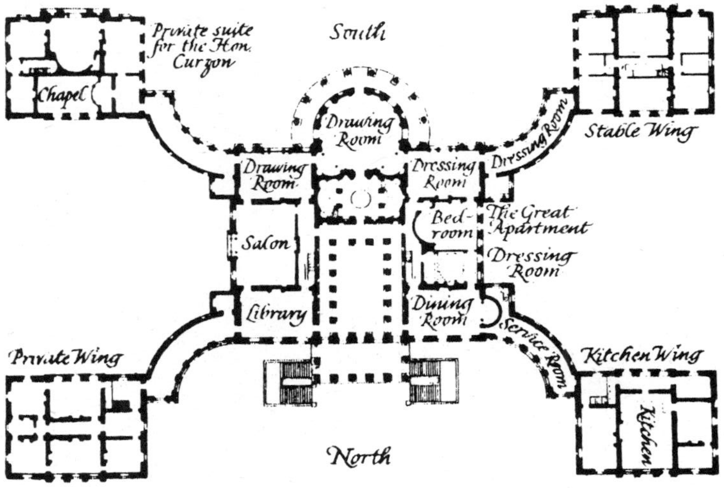

a

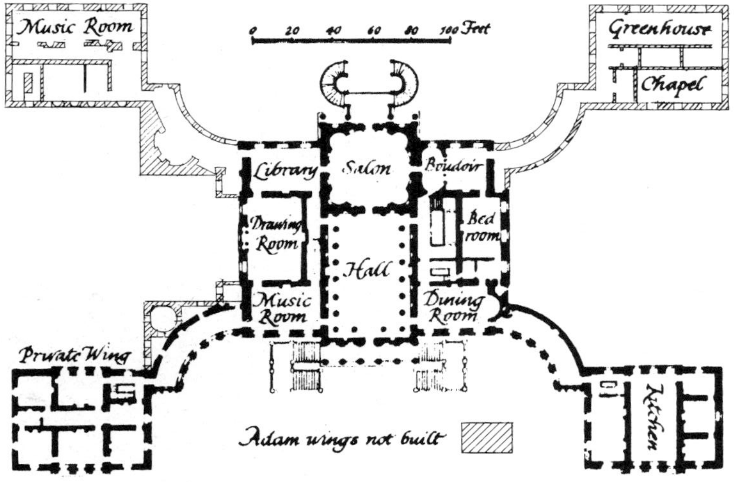

b

Figure 26 Kedleston Hall, Derbyshire, chimney piece in the marble hall by Robert Adam, *c* 1760. Photograph National Monuments Board, London.

Discussion

At first sight the two buildings are similar but as soon as we begin to compare them in detail there are many contrasts: the massing of the exterior is less staccato, though the wings of Adam's building were never erected. Instead of a temple front there is a Roman triumphal arch. Notice how the entablature breaks forward to reach the tops of the columns and is not treated like a beam; and see how the swags between the capitals increase the depth of the patterned band though they are not where a frieze strictly should be. The main difference in the decoration seems to be in the increasing unity of the whole scheme, though the motifs are more varied. At Holkham the rich bands of ornament on the ceiling contrast with the blank coffers of the vault, while at Kedleston coffering and ornament are combined and the roses in the niche echo those of the main dome. An ornamental entablature links the niche to the door, unlike Holkham, but it is not a pure classical entablature (compare fig 11 and the main entablature). The wall sconces are linked to the overall scheme with their little relief plaques. The Ionic capitals of the doorway are enriched. And compare the elegance and variety of ornament on the fireplace with Kent's more massive and architectural one (fig 22). Kedleston represents the arrival of Roman grandeur, freer, richer and more varied than before. Small wonder that in the next decade this style virtually swept the board.

Figure 27 Kedleston Hall, Derbyshire, the Marble Hall: Paine's grand palladian space with Robert Adam's neoclassical decoration. Photograph National Monuments Board, London.

4 Lacock Abbey, Wiltshire

Look at figs 28–31. What do they tell you about Lacock Abbey?

Discussion

The dining room with its strict Doric frieze (with ox heads) is Palladian classical but is in marked contrast to the extraordinary Gothick hall that lies next to it (you can see the windows of both rooms in fig 30). The gothick hall, though, is nothing like the real medieval gothic chapter house that also forms part of this unusual building. Lacock is an example of a house built into and onto a medieval nunnery at various times from the Reformation onwards. The owners had been staunch supporters of the Stuarts and so probably lacked the funds to indulge in major rebuilding in the eighteenth century. Nevertheless, some modernization was needed and the dining room was updated about 1740. Later, in 1754–55, Sanderson Miller, a talented amateur architect, was commissioned to rebuild the hall and produced one of the earliest pieces of Gothick work in the country. It provides a picturesque facade and a sensitive answer to the problems of additions to a building of such antiquity. The usual solution was to provide a completely new facade. The interior plaster work is delicate and elegant. Look at the curious niches with their specially commissioned terra cotta sculptures. The little turrets and open work parapet are especially frivolous and I particularly like the star shaped window. The style here is reduced to surface decoration (the basic form and structure of the old hall is largely untouched). This surface treatment is surely preferable to any continuation of the classical window pattern of the dining room alongside the unmistakably medieval buttresses.

Figure 28 Lacock Abbey, Wiltshire, the Dining Room. Photograph Country Life, London.

Figure 29 Lacock Abbey, Wiltshire, the Hall. Photograph Country Life, London.

Figure 30 Lacock Abbey, Wiltshire, the west (or entrance) front, photographed *c* 1849 by W. H. Fox Talbot.

Figure 31 Lacock Abbey, Wiltshire, the thirteenth-century chapterhouse. Photograph The National Trust, London.

5 Chiswick House, London

(Lord Burlington and William Kent *c* 1723–29)

Look at figs 32–35. How is this house different from the four we have studied so far?

Figure 32 Chiswick House, London, the villa entrance facade. Photograph Crown Copyright.

Discussion

I think the first thing is the scale, and of course the planning. Fig 33 also shows how the house was surrounded by elaborately varied gardens dotted with little buildings each of which housed sculpture or afforded shelter to strollers; but even the gardens are on a small scale for a noble house—less than half a mile from end to end. This in fact is as much a toy as a house and afforded a convenient country retreat from its owner's town mansion, Burlington House, Piccadilly.

You may have noticed that there is more to the house on the plan than is shown in fig 32. The actual villa is only an extension of an earlier house but it is kept distinct and separated by a link building (fig 33c). The villa is loosely based on a design by Palladio and displays programmatically the features of Palladianism. The order is Corinthian but restricted to the portico. The garden fronts have the so called 'Venetian' window as a central feature. The podium is clearly marked off as a basement and in fact there are no grand stairs inside, merely a first-floor connection with the old house. This is more a house for show than for living in. The ground floor housed Burlington's library and was a private sanctum. Above it were rooms for entertaining. At the centre of the building the octagonal domed hall rises right through the roof. All the other rooms are varied: round, square, octagonal and oblong but to a consistent set of proportions based on a square of roughly fifteen feet, the large rooms being around $1\frac{1}{4}$ or $1\frac{2}{3}$ of the square. The interior is richly decorated to the designs of Kent with some elements such as fireplaces consciously copied from Inigo Jones. Kent was also responsible for the gardens which are among the earliest examples of the new informal layout initiated by Bridgeman (compare fig 33 with fig 36). Another influence on the garden layout at Chiswick was Pope, who visited the villa frequently. He very probably influenced the layout of the gardens before the villa was built and wrote: 'Chiswick has been to me the finest thing this glorious sun has shined upon' (*Epistle to Lord Burlington*, iii 347).

Figure 33 (right) Chiswick House, London, plan of the gardens and views of the garden buildings. From Badeslade and Rocque *Vitruvius Britannicus*, vol IV (1736), plates 82 and 83. Photograph from the 1967 reprint by Benjamin Blom Books.

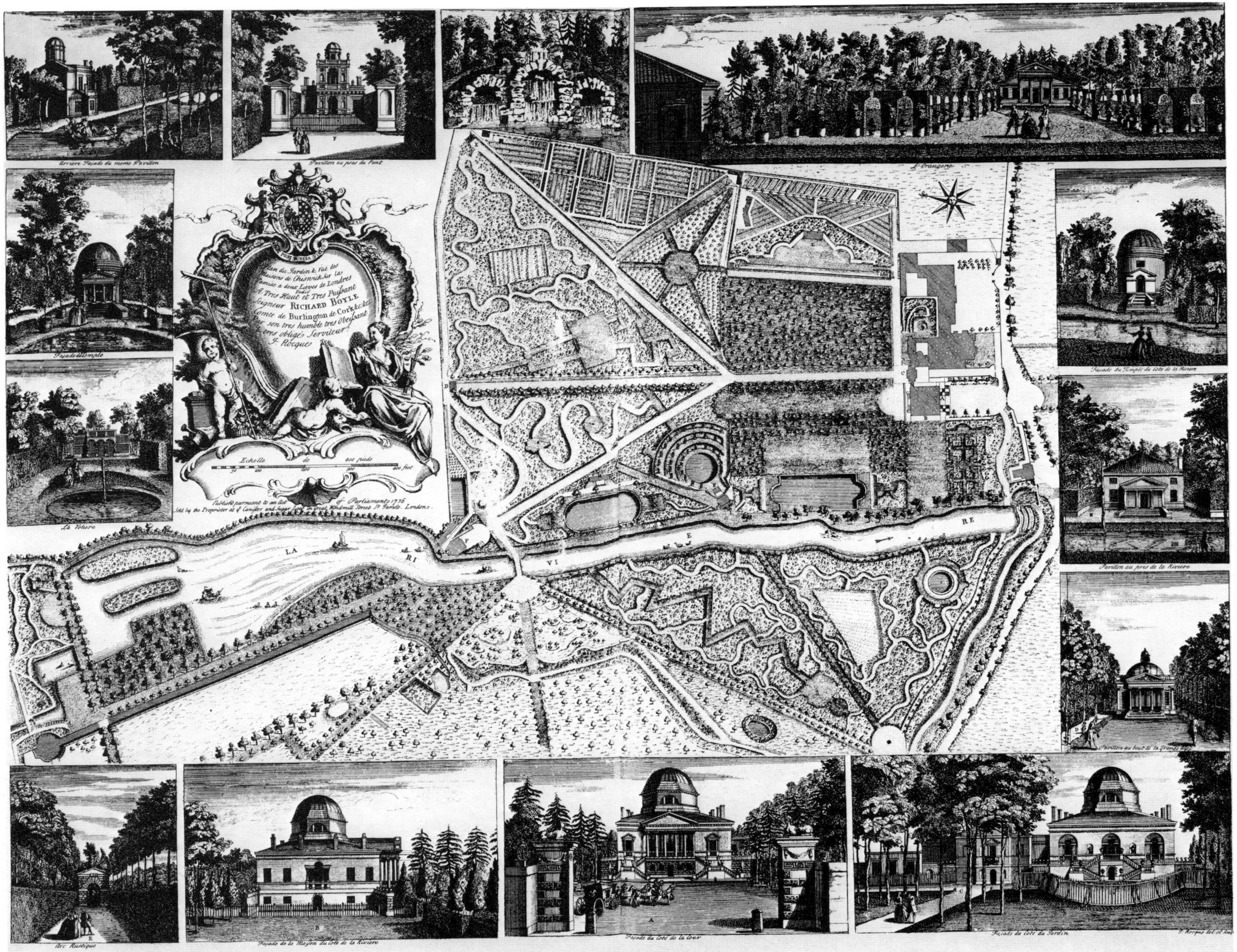
Plan du Jardin & Vüe des Maisons de Chiswick sur la Tamise a deux Lieves de Londres
Dedié A Tres Haut et Tres Puissant Seigneur RICHARD BOYLE Comte de Burlington de Cork &c. &c.
Par son tres humble tres Obeissant & tres obligé Serviteur J. Rocque
Echelle de 400 pieds
50 100 200 300 400 feet
Published pursuant to an Act of Parliament 1736
Sold by the Proprietor at ye Canister and Sugar Loaf in Great Windmill Street St James's. London.
LA RI VI E RE
Arriere Façade du meme Pavillon
Pavillon au pres du Pont
L'Orangerie
Façade du Temple
La Voliere
Pavillon au pres de la Riviere
Arc Rustique
Façade de la Maison du coté de la Riviere
Façade du coté de la Cour
Façade du coté du Jardin
J. Rocque del. et Sculp.

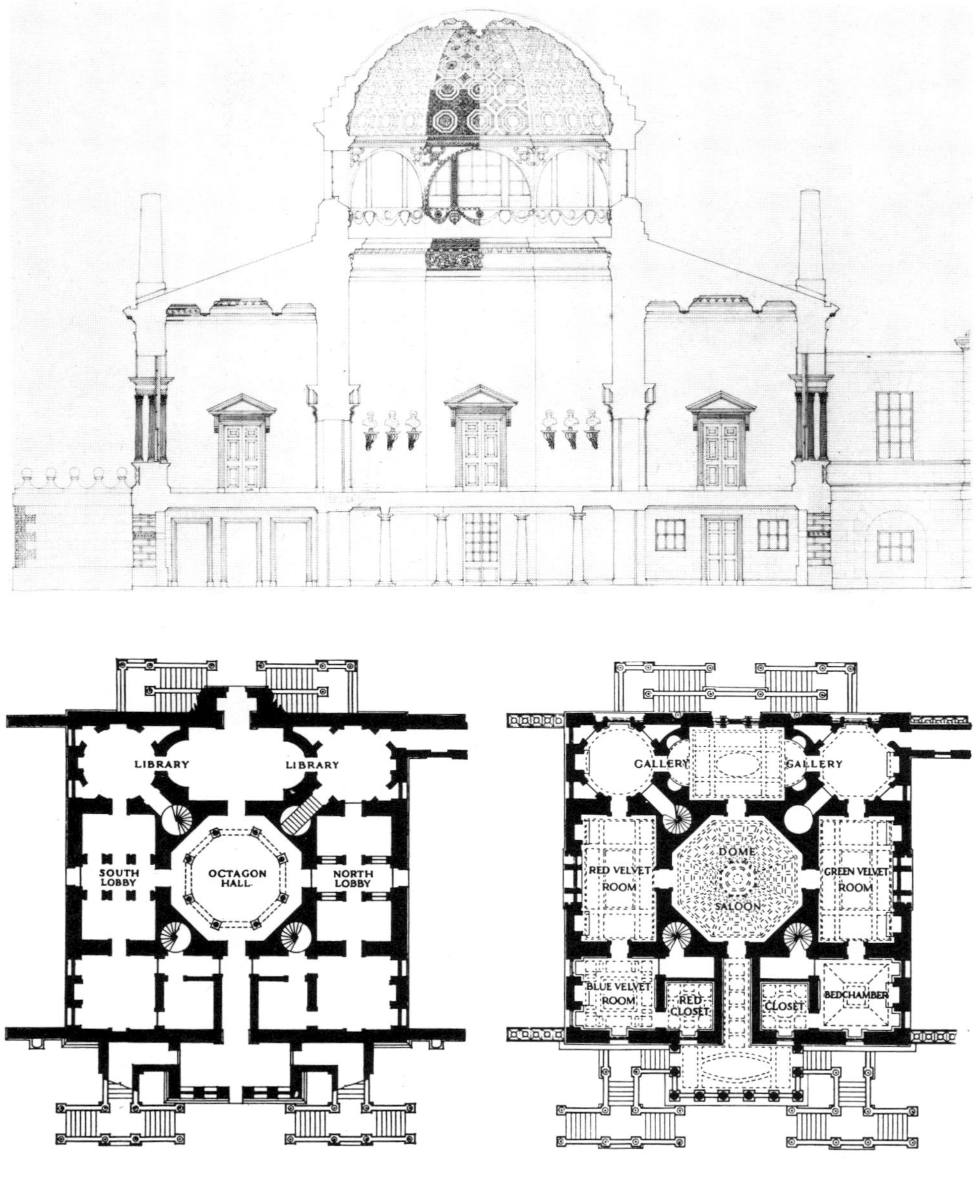

Figure 34 Chiswick House, London, section and plans. Photograph from J. Charlton *History and Description of Chiswick House and Gardens* (1978), tenth impression, HMSO. Crown Copyright.

Figure 35 Chiswick House, London, the gallery (compare fig 22). Photograph Crown Copyright.

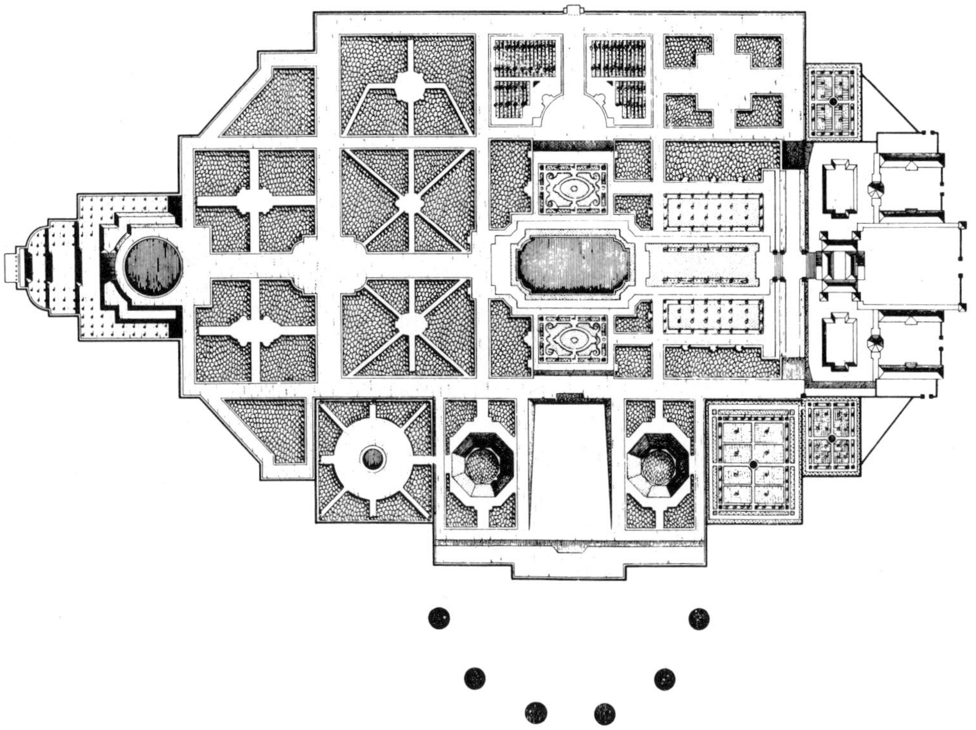

Figure 36 Eastbury Park, Dorset, Bridgeman's plan for the gardens, 1716, typifies the traditional formal layout. From Colen Campbell *Vitruvius Britannicus*, vol III (1725), plate 15. Photograph from 1967 reprint by Benjamin Blom Books.

Figure 37 Lancelot 'Capability' Brown's plan for Bowood, Wiltshire, 1763, shows the planned circuits and the use of lakes serpentine lines and belts and isolated clumps of trees. a mansion, b stables, c drives, d lakes, e ride, f mausoleum by Robert Adam, g lodge and home farm. Photograph Country Life, London.

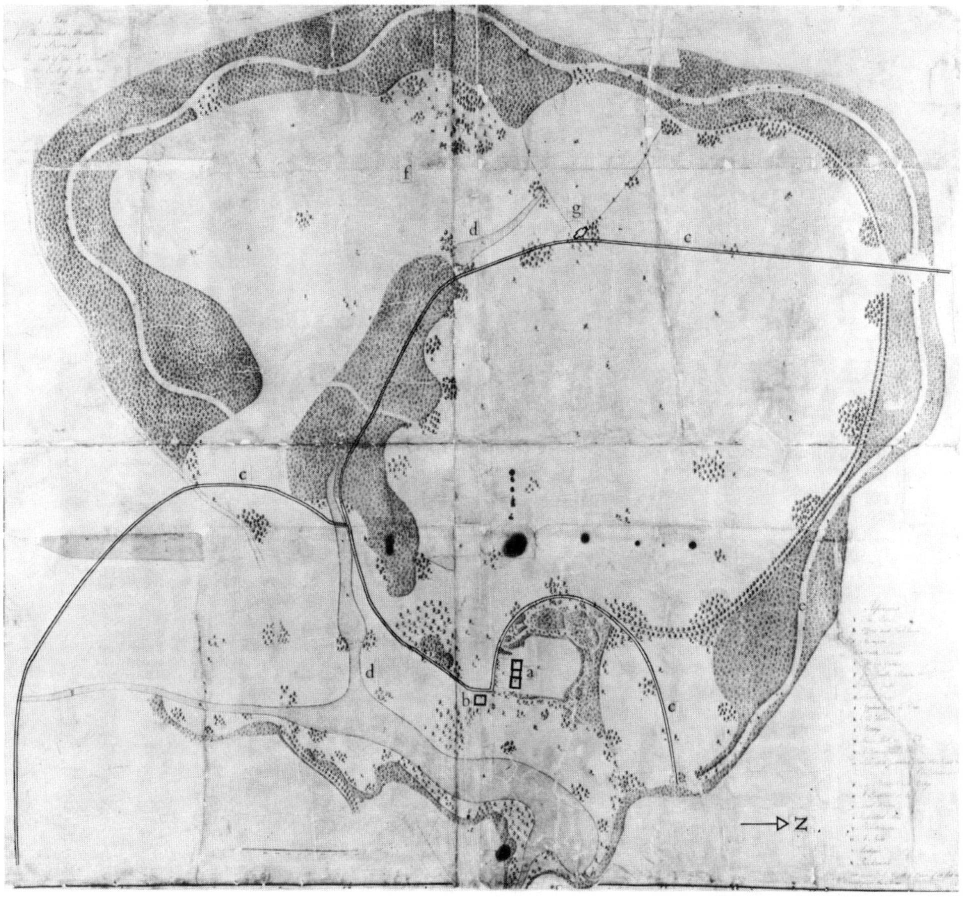

6 Stourhead and Shugborough

(Stourhead House, Colen Campbell 1721–23; grounds, Henry Flitcroft 1744 *ff.* Shugborough House, additions by ? Thomas Wright 1740s and James Stuart 1760s; Park monuments by James Stuart 1761 *ff.*)

These two houses provide outstanding examples of the eighteenth century ordered park in relation to the house. Look carefully at figs 38–46 and plate 1 noticing the variety and placing of buildings, clumps of trees and water. Try to work out where different views are taken from and how they relate to each other. The Stourhead gardens follow almost a generation after the building of the Palladian mansion. (fig 3). The scheme involved damming the river Stour to provide a large lake. The original village and church stand by its shore and the circuit of the lake (about one hour's stroll) is punctuated by classical buildings, furnished with sculpture and texts from Vergil, and a number of Gothic monuments transplanted from Bristol. There are also rustic structures such as the grotto and the bridge and tunnel over the concealed road. Several of the buildings have subsequently been demolished though those remaining are fine enough; yet beautiful as it is, this is a carefully contrived piece of landscape design and the vistas all carefully composed (note the lines of sight marked on the plan). The Palladian bridge only crosses a short arm of the lake not a stream, and moods are carefully engineered. The whole village and valley are turned into a visual pleasure ground. There was also an outer circuit for driving or riding, punctuated with vistas and monuments such as the 160-feet-high

Figure 38 Stourhead, Wiltshire, a plan of the gardens by Piper, 1779, though not fully accurate, it shows the original buildings and indicates the view lines. The rustic cottage (fig 41) is not shown, nor is the original village, parts of which were allowed to remain. Key: 1 house, 2 lawn, 3 obelisk, 4 100 feet wooden Palladian bridge, 5 ?Turkish Tent (demolished), 6 statue of Apollo Belvedere (removed), 7 grotto, 8 rustic work (demolished), 9 Chinese alcove (demolished), 10 terrace walk, 11 Ionic temple, 12 Pantheon, 13 Temple of Flora, 14 building now demolished, ?site of Chinese Ombrello, 15 dam, 17 rockwork bridge, 17 stone bridge, 18 part of village, 19 Hermitage (demolished), 20 Temple of Apollo, 21 grotto and underpass, 22 Bristol cross (background building not erected). Photograph Kungl Akademien för de fria Konsterna, Stockholm.

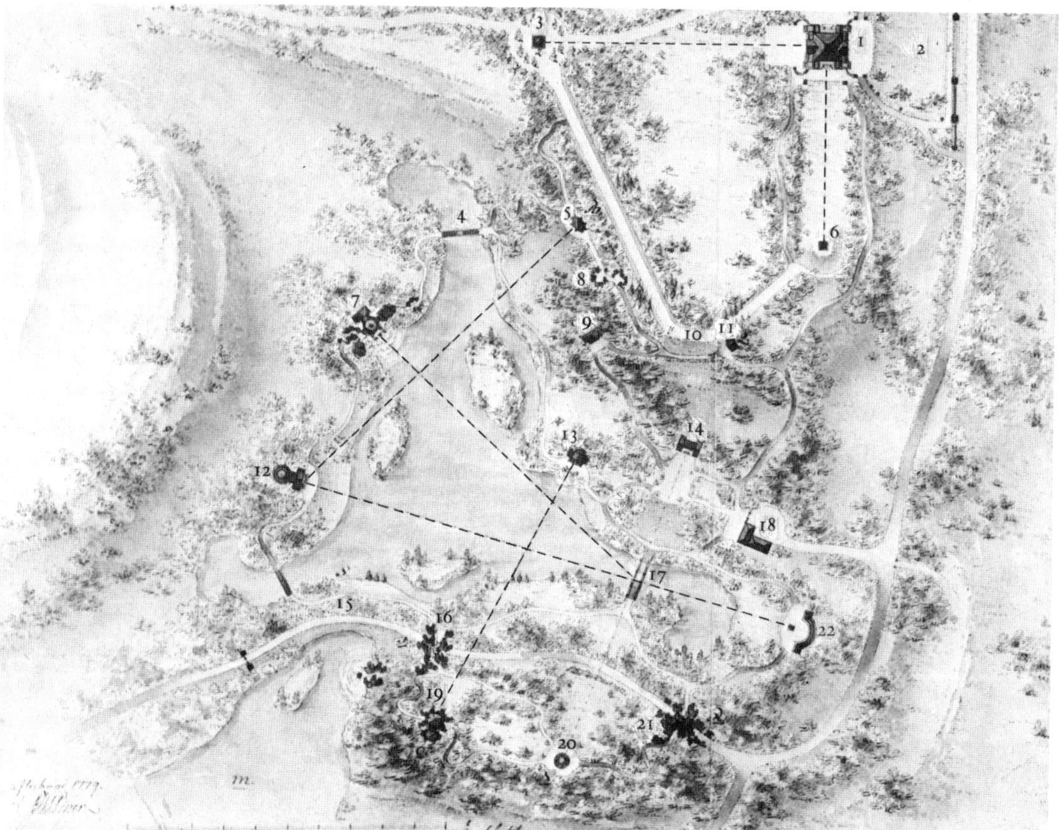

Figure 39 Stourhead, Wiltshire, drawing of the gardens by C. W. Bampfylde, *c* 1775, showing the grounds as they were originally. Photograph The National Trust, London.

Figure 40 Stourhead, Wiltshire, the English scene, the view from the Pantheon (compare fig 38). a Temple of Flora, b–e English scene: b part of village, c Bristol Cross, d Church, e bridge. Photograph Edwin Smith.

Figure 41 Stourhead, Wiltshire, inside the grotto. Photograph Edwin Smith.

triangular Alfred's Tower (1772). It is a far cry from such working estates as Holkham and except for a few sheep at pasture the actual agriculture is kept carefully out of sight.

Shugborough Park is less picturesque, because more altered, but reveals a similar attitude. It was the property of Thomas Anson a founder member of the Society of Dilettanti, a man of wide education and interests and a noted Whig. He was able to make extensive improvements through the wealth of his younger brother Admiral George Lord Anson whose fortune he inherited in 1762. He extended his estate by judiciously buying up the surrounding land and the village of Shugborough, most of which he removed to create his ornamental park. (Throughout the eighteenth century however the main Stafford to Lichfield road still ran through the park. Presumably the occasional cart provided a suitably interesting accent in the picture.)

Figure 42 Shugborough Park, Staffordshire, the house park and monuments by N. Dall, *c* 1769. a Arch of Hadrian, b Tower of the Winds, c Lanthorn of Demosthenes, d Pagoda, e Stafford road and bridge, f village. Photograph by Cliff Gutteridge, reproduced by courtesy of the Staffordshire County Museum, Shugborough.

Figure 43 Shugborough Park, Staffordshire, Palladian bridge and cascade (now demolished), in a sketch by Moses Griffiths, *c* 1762. Photograph by Cliff Gutteridge, reproduced by courtesy of the Staffordshire County Museum, Shugborough.

Figure 44 Shugborough Park, Staffordshire, Tower of the Winds, 1765 (altered 1805). Photograph A. F. Kersting, London.

Figure 45 Shugborough Park, Staffordshire, Lanthorn of Demosthenes, 1764–71. Phoograph by Cliff Gutteridge, reproduced by courtesy of the Staffordshire County Museum.

Figure 46 Lanthorn of Demosthenes, now known as the choragic monument of Lysicrates, Athens, *c* 334 BC. Photograph from Stuart and Revett *Antiquities of Athens*, 1762, vol I, Cep IV, plate III.

The general arrangement, like Stourhead and most other eighteenth-century layouts, involved a lake, here created by enlarging a mill pond. The earliest monuments were the Chinese house (1742) and a pagoda (1752) which reflect Admiral Anson's interest in the far east. The park buildings which include ruins, temples and monuments as well as the Chinese buildings, were all carefully sited to catch the eye. Three of the surviving monuments are by James Stuart and particularly interesting for their connection with contemporary scholarship. The Tower of the Winds (1765), The Triumphal Arch (1761) and the Lanthorn of Demosthenes (1764–1771) are all closely based on monuments in Athens first illustrated in Stuart and Revett's *Antiquities of Athens*, published by the Society of Dilettanti in 1762. Compare figs 45 and 46 to see how closely the originals are copied. But there was more than mere archaeology involved; Anson was in touch with Matthew Boulton and Josiah Wedgwood, two self-made men in the forefront of emerging industrialization, and both were involved in making the ornamental tripod on top of the Lanthorn of Demosthenes.

You may like to look through the *Gazetteer* now and see if you can find any houses listed there that show particular parallels to those we have discussed. If you can manage to visit any of the country houses listed you will find it enhances your study of this material.

Conclusion

You should now have formed some ideas about the architectural achievement of the eighteenth century. How would you sum up the qualities shown in the country houses you have studied?

Discussion

I find I am most impressed by the elegance and refinement of proportion and by the ordered splendour of the interiors. What also comes to mind is the almost conscious artificiality of this high-class life, so very far removed from the more down-to-earth middle classes and lesser gentry like Squire Western. The immense wealth needed to build a Holkham, a Chiswick or a Stourhead presupposed an extensive pyramid of property and wealth of which this unit has only presented the tip. Yet such was the power of eighteenth-century class structure that the great classical buildings and their details were copied with diminishing elaboration well down the social scale. Small houses of the eighteenth century are everywhere and their human proportions make them a delight to look at. Often these houses, and sometimes even their greater prototypes, were not well built, for in this age of reason it was emphatically the shape and not the substance of the structures that was admired. Yet eighteenth-century architecture has left us a legacy of elegance in space and design that has yet to be surpassed.

Selected bibliography

G. Beard *The Work of Robert Adam* (1978), John Bartholomew. This book combines a good brief introduction with an extensive bibliography and a fine series of plates.

M. R. Brownell *Alexander Pope and the Arts of Georgian England* (1978), Clarendon Press. A detailed study that covers Pope's great influence on the development of garden design.

H. Colvin *A Biographical Dictionary of British Architects 1600–1840* (1978), John Murray. An indispensable work of reference.

H. Colvin and J. Harris (eds) *The Country Seat, Studies in the History of the British Country House, Essays presented to Sir John Summerson* (1970), Penguin. A collection of essays on a wide range of topics many of which relate to eighteenth-century houses.

T. Davis *The Gothic Taste* (1974) David and Charles. A readable and fully informative account of gothick architecture in the eighteenth and early nineteenth centuries.

J. Fleming *Robert Adam and his Circle in Edinburgh and Rome*, (1962), John Murray. Packed with detail this book is invaluable for the way in which it relates Adam and his work to the circle of clients and friends.

M. Girouard *Life in the English Country House (A Social and Architectural History)* (1978), Yale University Press. A readable and well illustrated book that effectively relates the styles of architecture to their functions.

C. Hussey *English Country Houses, Early Georgian 1715–1760, Mid-Georgian 1760–1800* (1955), Country Life. Studies of individual houses beautifully illustrated and with excellent introductory essays.

M. Jourdain *The Work of William Kent* (1948), Country Life. The standard biography of this architect.

J. Lees Milne *Earls of Creation* (1962), Hamish Hamilton. An enjoyable book about four great patrons including Lord Burlington and Lord Pembroke.

N. Pevsner *The Buildings of England*, Penguin. A county-by-county series provides detailed descriptions of all the major buildings and notes the minor ones. Invaluable for any visitor to a country house. (Parallel series are being produced by other authors for Scotland, Wales and Northern Ireland.)

J. Rykwert *The First Moderns: Architecture between Descartes and Newton* (1980), MIT Press. A full and scholarly account of the workings of the architectural profession and patronage during the period.

D. Stroud *Capability Brown* (1975), Faber. An exhaustive study of Brown's work as landscape designer and architect.

H. E. Stutchbury *The Architecture of Colen Campbell* (1967), Manchester University Press. The best recent study of this prime Palladian architect.

J. Summerson *Architecture in Britain 1530–1830* (1953), Penguin. By far the best architectural history of the period as a whole. This book is both detailed and readable and very perceptive in its comments.

H. A. Tipping *English Houses, Period V Vol I 1714–1760* and *Period VI Vol I 1760–1820* (1921), Country Life. A series of detailed and well illustrated studies of many of the buildings studied.

P. Willis *Charles Bridgman and the English Landscape Garden* (1978), Zwemmer. A lavish and detailed study of the rise of the 'English garden' which sets Bridgman in relation to the work of other artists and literati of the mid eighteenth century.

R. Wittkower *Palladio and English Palladianism* (1974), Thames & Hudson. A collection of stimulating essays tracing the influence of a style with an excellent treatment of the contemporary publications.

D. Yarwood *The Architecture of England* (1963), Batsford. Quite a clear and useful survey with many drawings.

Part 2 Landscape Painting and the Work of Thomas Gainsborough

Introduction: Landscape Gardening and Landscape Painting

In Part 1 Colin Cunningham discussed 'the move away from the intellectual to the romantic' in the evolution of country-house architecture, citing the influence of developments in landscape gardening. In the following section I shall look at some of these developments in relation to contemporary fashions in landscape painting.

In the seventeenth century art theorists[16] suggested a close relationship between poetry and painting, a notion probably inspired by the Roman poet Horace's famous simile '*Ut pictura poesis*' (poetry is like painting). Seventeenth-century theorists saw the two disciplines as similar in content, use of imagery and purpose. During the early eighteenth century landscape gardening was added to poetry and painting to form the trilogy of the 'sister arts'. This concept inspired Horace Walpole's much quoted notion of 'the three new graces'. As a poet and art critic with an interest in architecture and landscape gardening, Walpole encouraged the 'modern' view that these three disciplines were interrelated, although he was not, of course, implying that poetry and painting were new art forms.

Walpole's 'three new graces' were anticipated in the theories and interests of Alexander Pope, whose *Essay on Man* you studied in Unit 3. With some essays published in the *Guardian* in 1713, Pope won a reputation as a critic of topiary[17] art and the formal school of landscape gardening. Horace Walpole's own essay *On Modern Gardening* (Course Anthology Vol 2) cites Pope as an influence on William Kent, the designer of the gardens at Chiswick Park (fig 33), Houghton Hall, Stowe and Rousham.

It was probably to Kent that Pope made his reported statement:

> All gardening is landscape painting; you may distance things by darkening them and by narrowing towards the end, in the same manner as they do in painting.
>
> *Spence's Anecdotes* (1820), p. 144

Pope believed that a painter's skills could be of value to a landscape gardener, that it was necessary to 'paint as you plant' (see p. 16).

The collaboration of the sister arts must be seen in relation to contemporary attitudes towards 'nature'. Apart from its various non-painterly meanings[18], nature had at least two different meanings to artists and painters in the early eighteenth

[16] The French painter Du Fresnoy published a poem in 1688 called 'De Arte Graphica' which linked poetry and painting together. This was translated into English by Dryden in 1695 and became very popular in England.

[17] 'Topiary' was a seventeenth-century style of gardening which involved cutting shrubs and bushes into ornamental shapes.

[18] Pope, for example, uses the phrase 'Nature's peace' to describe the harmony of the created world (see text of *An Essay on Man* IV 55–6 in the supplementary material for Unit 3).

century. It could mean 'common nature', the ordinary visible world around us. It could also represent an ideal Nature with moral or religious connotations—an improvement on the visible world. Sir Joshua Reynolds (1723–92), who became first president of the Royal Academy in 1769, believed that through art one should seek to attain a morally uplifting ideal Nature; although he often used the word in both senses. In a discourse delivered to the Royal Academy in 1786, he uses the term in its first sense to show its *opposition* to the 'Art of Gardening':

> So also Gardening, as far as Gardening is an Art, or entitled to that appellation, is a deviation from nature; for if the true taste consists, as many hold, in banishing every appearance of Art, or any traces of the footsteps of men, it would then be no longer a Garden.

Although Reynolds was not in sympathy with the idea that the skills of painting should be adapted to landscape design, some of his views were not so far removed from those of Pope. An artful reinterpretation of nature was what Pope sought to copy from landscape painting, in particular from the idealized landscapes of popular seventeenth-century French and Italian painters such as Claude Lorrain (1600–82), Nicholas Poussin (1593/4–1665), his brother-in-law Gaspard Poussin (1615–75) and Salvator Rosa (1615–73). Engravings of the works of these artists were widely circulated in England by the 1720s and the original paintings were much sought after by wealthy collectors.

Landscapes by Rosa and paintings such as Claude's *Classical Landscape* (fig 47) provided a wealth of visual imagery inspired by the Campagna around Rome and Naples, which reminded the English gentleman of scenes which he believed he had seen on his Grand Tour. Rosa's wild rocky landscapes and Claude's peaceful wooded scenes inspired the gardens of several eighteenth-century stately homes.

Figure 47 Claude Lorrain, *Classical Landscape*, oil on canvas, 101.5 × 134 cm (40 × 52¾ ins). The Barber Institute of Fine Arts, University of Birmingham.

Notable examples are the gardens at Stourhead, Stowe (where part of the grounds were known as the 'Elysian Fields', a reference to Vergil's *Aeneid*) and Rousham, laid out in the 1740s (figs 38–40).

Pope was one of the first garden theorists to react against the artificial geometrical order of the formal Italian and French garden, which can be seen, for example, in Le Notre's garden at Versailles. In his own garden at Twickenham, which he started laying out in 1720, he introduced serpentine paths and irregular vistas. He also included many classical and allegorical associations in the form of urns, inscriptions, busts and statues. For this reason Pope's garden at Twickenham is often seen to represent a transition period in garden design when allegorical or 'poetic' references are combined with an apparent informality of design.

Many of the innovations that preoccupied Pope are discussed in Walpole's essay *On Modern Gardening*, which formed the final chapter of a history of painting, thus reinforcing the idea of collaboration between the arts. The essay marks an important step in the movement away from the formal garden towards irregular designs that follow more closely the disorder of nature itself. Walpole says of Kent's design for the grounds of Houghton Hall, Norfolk:

> And the garden in its turn was to be set free from its prim regularity, that it might assort with the wilder country without . . . He [Kent] leaped the fence and saw that all nature was a garden
>
> Course Anthology Vol 2, p. 83

But this did not mean, of course, that Kent could just leave the grounds as they were at Houghton. Kent's garden had to be rearranged to imitate the most desirable features from nature in a combination which perfectly suited the site in question. The garden must be 'painted' to look natural:

> Thus the pencil of his imagination bestowed all the arts of landscape on the scenes he handled. The great principles on which he worked were perspective light and shade. Groups of trees broke too uniform or too extensive a lawn.
>
> Course Anthology Vol 2, p. 83

In the mid eighteenth century, these painterly effects in garden design gradually became more important than the literary allusions evoked by the inclusion of statues or inscriptions. In the later landscape gardens of Capability Brown, such as the grounds at Longleat (laid out in 1760), most of the literary references have been replaced by undulating hills, winding paths and 'natural' vistas. Longleat was a garden that appealed to the *senses* rather than the intellect.

This change in attitude is paralleled in contemporary developments in aesthetic theory, in particular in the writings of Joseph Addison, whose essays *On Taste and the Pleasures of the Imagination* were published in the *Spectator* in 1711–12. He reflects the 'empiricist' view, associated with the British Enlightenment, that the imagination is first stirred by the senses rather than the intellect. You have already come across a similar attitude in *Tom Jones* (pp. 152 and 253; discussed in Units 4–5) when Fielding refers to 'Mr Lock's blind man', supporting Locke's view that our ideas of objects are derived through sense experience. Addison believed that the irregular careless forms of 'the common field' offer more direct stimulus to the imagination than the regular lines of a formal garden:

> There is something bold and masterly in the rough, careless strokes of nature, than in the nice touches and embellishments of art. The beauties of the most stately garden or palace lie in a narrow compass, the imagination runs them over . . . but in the wild fields of nature, the sight wanders up and down without confinement, and is fed with an infinite variety of images.
>
> Addison, Essay V

Addison's 'infinite variety of images' is not dissimilar to Walpole's 'Prospect, animated prospect' (Course Anthology Vol 2, p. 87). Both writers were concerned with the aesthetic stimulus offered by a view, rather than its intellectual meaning.

Figure 48 William Kent, *Pope's Garden, Twickenham, the Shell Temple*, drawing. Reproduced by courtesy of the Trustees of the British Museum.

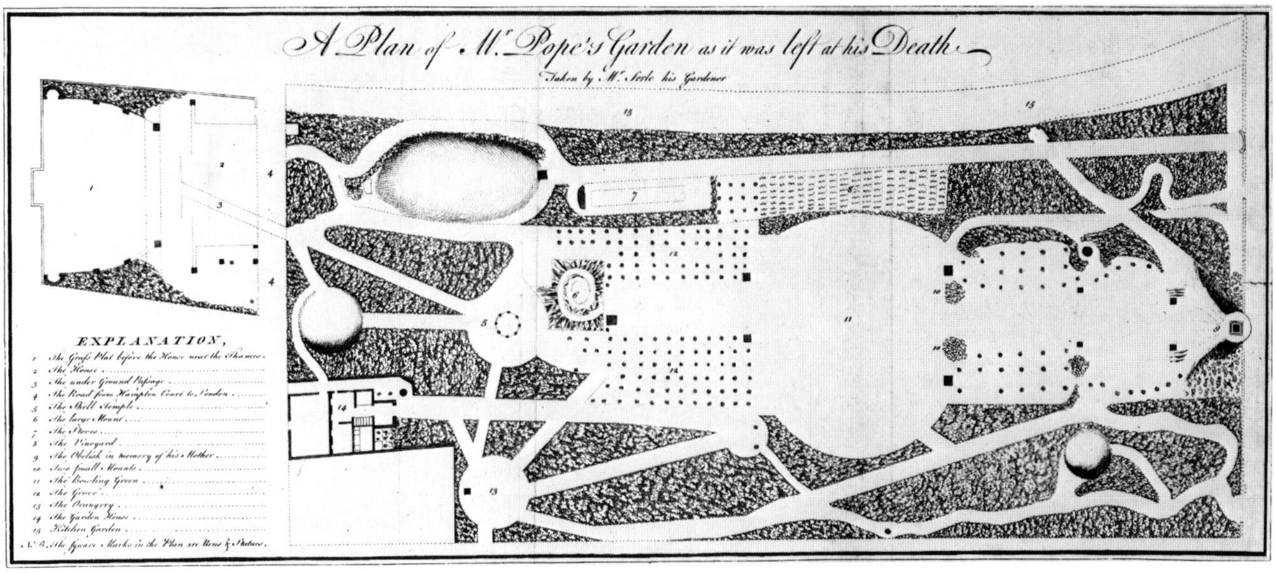

Figure 49. J. Serle, *Plan of Mr Pope's Garden at Twickenham.*

Exercise

Please read Walpole's essay *On Modern Gardening* in the *Course Anthology* Vol 2 and look at William Kent's drawing and Serle's plan of Pope's garden (figs 48 and 49). To what extent does the design of Pope's garden reflect the new ideas on gardening described in Walpole's essay? Are there any characteristics of the design, or of Walpole's written description of the garden, which suggest a close relationship with landscape painting?

Pope's garden (which disappeared in the nineteenth century and is now the site of a pub named 'Pope's Grotto') was situated on a five-acre site on the edge of the Thames. As you can see from figs 48 and 49 it included a grotto, a 'shell temple', made entirely from sea shells, three lawns which merged into each other, and was surrounded by thick woods.

Walpole singles out two main features from the garden: the variety of the scenery and the use of contrasts. He describes 'the passing through the gloom from the grotto to the opening day' and the 'retiring and again assembled shades'. This emphasis on light and shadow is borrowed from the techniques of painting, illustrated, for example in the chiaroscuro of a Claude landscape.

You can see from Serle's plan that Pope constructed artificial mounds (labelled no 10 in the key) to give the site an irregular undulating character. And anticipating Walpole's description of Kent's activities at Houghton, Pope used groups of trees to break up the lawn. Similarly, groves of trees were often used to break otherwise monotonous vistas in landscapes by Claude or Gaspar Poussin.

But I expect you also noticed that it would be a mistake to identify 'Pope's Grotto' too closely with the style of 'modern' gardening which Walpole praises in his essay. Although each part of the garden varies in character from the rest, there are many aspects of the design which echo the regularity of a formal French garden. The quincunx groves[19] are arranged in ordered parallel rows and many of the main paths follow straight lines. The combination of irregular and regular elements could be seen as part of Pope's attempt to create variety and contrasts, but it separates him from Kent's ruling principle 'that nature abhors a straight line'[20].

Pope's poetic garden incorporated layers of allegorical meaning—both literary and personal—into its 'painted' vistas. Kent's drawing gives you some idea of the wealth of ornament and statues which were crowded into the site. The whole garden was designed around the theme of motherhood and Pope's own mother was commemorated in the obelisk (no 9 on the plan). The grotto and underground passage were furnished with geological specimens, shells, bits of glass and other ornaments with personal associations.

It seems curious that Walpole, with his commitment to the free and painterly style of gardening of William Kent, was not more critical of the traditional characteristics of Pope's garden, concentrating on the features that parallel the skills of painting. I think that the selective nature of Walpole's comments was partly dictated by the tastes of the period in which he was writing his history of 'modern' gardening (first published in 1771 at the printing office in his 'Gothick' villa at Strawberry Hill). Walpole selected from Pope's garden those features which seemed to him to anticipate contemporary developments in the sister arts. In the 1770s these were epitomized in the landscape gardens of Capability Brown, or the so-called 'picturesque' landscape paintings of Thomas Gainsborough.

One of my main aims in the following pages is to show the extent to which developments in Gainsborough's landscape paintings mirror those in English eighteenth century landscape gardening. While I am not suggesting that Gainsborough's paintings were *directly* influenced by innovations in landscape gardening, I hope to show how these painted landscapes reflect similar tastes in design, composition and attitudes to nature.

[19] Groves of trees or bushes arranged in groups of five in which four occupy the corners with the fifth in the centre.

[20] Walpole makes this comment in his essay. However, even he admits that this principle can be taken too far and that there can be some aesthetic value in using straight lines in particular situations.

Thomas Gainsborough: a brief biographical outline

1727	Baptized on 14 May in Sudbury, Suffolk
(?) 1740	Went to London and became pupil of Hubert François Gravelot, a French engraver
1746	Married Margaret Burr
1748	Returned to Sudbury with his wife, and started to earn his living as a painter
1752	Moved from Sudbury to Ipswich
1758	Travelled around the Midlands, painting commissioned portraits
1759	Moved from Ipswich to Bath
1760	Exhibited at the Society of Arts
1766	Moved to a house in the Circus, Bath
1768	Became a founder member of the Royal Academy
1772	His nephew, Gainsborough Dupont, became his assistant
1773	Objected to the placing of his pictures at the Royal Academy annual exhibition, and did not exhibit again until 1777
1774	Moved from Bath to London, establishing himself in a house on Pall Mall
1783	Toured the Lake District in the summer
1784	Objected again to the hanging of his pictures at the Royal Academy exhibition, and began a series of annual exhibitions in his own studio in Pall Mall
1788	Died on 2 August

1 Gainsborough and Reynolds: Painterly and 'Poetical' Representation

In his fourteenth *Discourse* (Course Anthology Vol 2), written in 1788, four months after the death of Gainsborough, Sir Joshua Reynolds wrote:

> If Gainsborough did not look at nature with a poet's eye, it must be acknowledged that he saw her with the eye of a painter, and gave a faithful, if not poetical representation of what he had before him.

Reynolds is using the term 'poetical' in the same sense in which I have been using the word 'poetic' to describe Pope's garden, to denote an artificial reconstruction of nature with literary associations.

As first president of the Royal Academy, founded in 1768, Reynolds supported (in theory at least) the principle that art is an activity of the *mind*, achieved through the application of learned knowledge, which should result in what he called the 'Grand Manner', a style particularly suitable for history painting. In his first *Discourse* he insisted that:

> An implicit obedience to the Rules of Art, as established by the practice of the great Masters should be exacted from the young students; that these models, which have passed through the approbation of ages, should be considered by them as perfect and infallible guides.[21]

Reynolds seems to be encouraging a kind of eclecticism, a style of art which is shaped through the study of great masters. High up on Reynold's own list of respected masters we would find the Greek sculptor Phidias, Michelangelo and Raphael, closely followed by Rembrandt and Rubens. The works of these artists were models from which the student could learn to improve on nature. Reynolds believed that it should be closely studied, but that simple copying of nature did not constitute a great art which would 'raise and enlarge conceptions' (*Discourse* III; quoted in Eitner, p. 37).

He attributed to Gainsborough the eye of a painter rather than a poet because his work seemed to represent the antithesis of the 'Grand Manner'. Gainsborough was well-known to be anti-intellectual[22] and his works are relatively free of literary or allegorical references. In a light-hearted reply to his close friend William Jackson, who had suggested that he might consider including historical figures in his landscapes, Gainsborough wrote:

> I admire your notions of most things and do agree with you that there might be exceeding pretty Pictures painted of the kind you mention. But are you sure you don't mean instead of the Flight into Egypt, my flight out of Bath! Do you consider my dear maggoty Sir, what a deal of work History Pictures require to what little dirty subjects of coal horses and jackasses and such figures as I fill up with.
>
> Quoted in M. Woodall *The Letters of Thomas Gainsborough* (1963), Cupid Press; no 49, p. 99

[21] L. Eitner *Neoclassicism and Romanticism, 1750–1850* vol 1 (1971), p. 35. Eitner includes useful excerpts from several discourses. A complete edition of the *Discourses* has been published by Yale University Press 1976.

[22] William Jackson in *The Four Ages*, London 1798, has claimed that Gainsborough 'scarcely ever read a book' and that he deliberately avoided the company of literary men (Jackson was a vicar and an organist with whom Gainsborough had regular correspondence.)

Figure 50 Thomas Gainsborough, *River Scene with Figures and Dog barking at a Swallow*, *c* 1747, oil on canvas, 76 × 151 cm (30 × 59½ ins). National Gallery of Scotland, Edinburgh.

If we compare the figures in Gainsborough's early landscape painting *River Scene with Figures and Dog barking at a Swallow*, *c* 1747 (fig 50) with the carefully posed pseudo-classical figures in Claude's *Classical Landscape* (fig 47) it is not difficult to see how, comparatively speaking, Gainsborough's figures might appear to be 'little dirty subjects'. While the Claude has all the trappings of a 'poetic' subject, Gainsborough's painting is closer to 'common nature'.

Gainsborough could also be more direct in his opposition to the principles advocated by Sir Joshua Reynolds and the Academicians.[23] In reply to a Mr Hoare, who had sent him a copy of Reynold's fourth *Discourse*, Gainsborough conveys his personal view on the 'Grand Manner':

> Mr. Gainsborough's Respects to Mr. Hoare, and is much obliged for the sight of Sir Joshua's Discourse which he thinks amazingly clever, and cannot be too much admired (together with its Ingenious Author) by every candid lover of the Art. The truth of what he observes concerning Fresco, and the Great style, Mr. G. is convinced of by what he had often heard Mr. Hoare say of the works of Rafaelle and Michel Angelo—But betwixt Friends Sir Joshua either forgets, or does not chuse see that his Instruction is all adapted to form the History Painter, which he must know there is no call for in this country. The Ornamental style (as he calls it) seems form'd for Portraits . . . Every one knows that the grand style [which is suitable for history painting] must consist in plainness and simplicity, and that silks and satins, Pearls and trifling ornaments would be as hurtful to simplicity, as flourishes in a Psalm tune.

But Gainsborough finds that he cannot support the Grand Style, believing:

> . . . there must be a variety of lively touches and surprizing Effect to make the heart dance, or else they [Reynold's pictures] had better be done in a church—so in portrait painting there must be a Lustre and finishing to bring it up to individual life.
>
> Woodall, no 46, p. 95, undated

As we can infer from Gainsborough's reply, Reynolds had shown how the Grand Style, with its emphasis on simplicity and precise finish, was particularly suitable for history painting. He had contrasted it with the inferior ornamental style which concentrates on surface effects (Gainsborough calls it 'a variety of lively touches and surprising Effects') and appeals to the sense of sight. Gainsborough, on the other hand, extols the suitability of the ornamental style which concentrates on the textures of rich fabrics and jewels, for portrait painting.

His remark that there is no call for history painting in this country is an indirect reference to the ambiguities within the Royal Academy. Despite the President's principles as expounded in his *Discourses*, the institution failed to create a coherent school of history painting. Members included many portrait and genre artists. Those Academicians who did devote their careers to history painting (such as Gavin Hamilton 1723–98 or Benjamin West 1739–1820) often found it difficult to find commissions for their works. Patrons in eighteenth-century England were more interested in less elevated styles of portrait, genre, and to a lesser extent landscape and still life painting. Ironically, portraits formed a major part of Reynolds' work, and Gainsborough himself was one of the founder members of the Royal Academy. Despite disagreements over the hanging of his paintings, he exhibited regularly at Academy exhibitions between 1769 and 1784.

Exercise

Bearing in mind the points of view discussed above, please read Reynold's fourteenth *Discourse* (Course Anthology Vol 2) and look carefully at Reynold's

[23] When the Royal Academy was founded by George III in 1768, the initial membership totalled 38 painters. Some of the better known Academicians included Benjamin West, Thomas Sandby, Richard Wilson, Francis Hayman, William Chambers and Nathaniel Dance.

portrait of *Mrs Siddons as the Tragic Muse*, 1784 (Course Anthology, Vol 2, Plate 13) and Gainsborough's portrait of *Mrs Richard Brinsley Sheridan*, 1785 (fig 51).

1 Compare the subject matter and style of these two paintings. Can you identify any symbolic references in the Reynolds? Do these make any difference to the total effect of this painting as compared with the Gainsborough?

2 In view of my comments so far on both painters' attitudes towards the 'Grand Manner', can you find any contradictions in the fourteenth *Discourse*?

Figure 51 Thomas Gainsborough, *Mrs Richard Brinsley Sheridan, née Elizabeth Linley*, painted spring 1785, slightly altered winter 1786, oil on canvas, 147.5 × 119.5 cm (58 × 47 ins). Andrew Mellon Collection, National Gallery of Art, Washington.

1 These are both commissioned portraits, painted within one year of each other. Mrs Sheridan is a relatively straightforward portrait, while Mrs Siddons is presented as the 'tragic muse', a reference which may seem to be slightly absurd to us, but which would have been easily understood by an eighteenth-century audience. Mrs Siddons was an actress and her disguise is a direct reference to classical Greek tragedy. The background comprises two symbolic figures carrying the cup and the dagger, traditional emblems of Melpomene, the tragic muse. The compositional organization and Mrs Siddons' pose, probably derived from the prophets on Michelangelo's Sistine Chapel ceiling, add an air of religious awe to the scene.

Mrs Sheridan, on the other hand, shares none of the symbolic trappings of her contemporary, the 'tragic muse'. Mrs Sheridan's aspirations appear to be relatively terrestrial. She is seated on the ground instead of a quasi-sacred throne and her background is a simple landscape setting. In contrast with the more formal, symmetrical position of Mrs Siddons, she is sitting to one side of the composition in a relatively informal pose.

You will probably have noticed how Gainsborough's portrait seems to put more emphasis on the process of painting; his brushwork has an almost sketchy texture. Mrs Sheridan's dress, her soft curling hair and her gauze scarf are all painted with a loose sketchiness. This style of brushwork is echoed in the treatment of the trees and the surrounding ground. There is little formal difference between the figure and her landscape setting. The figure appears to be 'enveloped'[24] by the landscape, which is not merely a background setting but a study in its own right.[25]

According to Gainsborough's daughter Margaret he achieved his painterly effects by mixing his oil paints with turpentine, creating a thin, flowing paint texture. But this was only one stage in the evolution of an oil painting. He would first prime the canvas with a luminous, yellowish film of paint, upon which he would sketch out the composition. He would then build up several layers of colour, taking enormous care over the thickness and quality of his paint. Thus the final impression of sketchiness was, in fact, the product of a lengthy and painstaking process.

Although Gainsborough and Reynolds have interpreted their subjects in rather different ways, one could argue that *both* artists have idealized their clients. This is immediately obvious in the exalted status of Mrs Siddons as a 'tragic muse'. Gainsborough's emphasis on surface textures contributes to a romanticized image of Mrs Sheridan. She is seated gracefully under a tree, in a position which is echoed by the diagonal flow of the brushstrokes, and her slightly tilted head is framed by the gauze scarf which ripples in a gentle breeze.

On occasion, Reynolds also painted portrait subjects against landscape backgrounds, although these landscapes were often part of the literary or historical references suggested by the subject.[26] In contrast, Gainsborough enjoyed painting and sketching landscapes in their own right. He found it quite difficult to sell these works because eighteenth century patrons were generally more interested in commissioning portraits, and within academic circles landscape was regarded as an inferior genre. In a letter to William Jackson he wrote:

> I'm sick of portraits and wish very much to take up my Viol da Gamba and walk off to some sweet Village where I can paint Landskips and enjoy the fag end of life in quietness and ease.
>
> Woodall, no 56, p. 115

[24] J. Hayes *Gainsborough* (1975), Phaidon, p. 225, note 119.
[25] In his use of informal landscape backgrounds Gainsborough was influenced by the portraits of Sir Anthony Van Dyck (1599–1641), a Flemish artist who become official court painter to James I.
[26] As in, for example, Reynolds' portrait of *Commodore Keppel* (1753–54), National Maritime Museum, Greenwich. The Commodore's pose is probably a reference to the Apollo Belvedere, and the rugged seacoast in the background is a reference to the Commodore's own career at sea.

2 Reynolds' praise of Gainsborough in the fourteenth *Discourse* seems to involve a certain amount of intellectual confusion. Gainsborough's lack of 'Academic' training, his choice of subjects and his technique were, in a sense, in direct opposition to the principles set out in the earlier discourses. Reynolds was clearly captivated by Gainsborough's painterly 'effects', commenting:

> It must be allowed that this hatching manner of Gainsborough did very much contribute to the lightness of effect which is so eminent a beauty in his pictures! . . . and he had . . . 'truly a painter's eye for colouring'.
>
> Course Anthology Vol 2, p. 99

But as Reynolds himself points out, this 'peculiarity of style' was the feature which many considered Gainsborough's greatest defect, presumably because it was opposed to the precise finish favoured by the Academicians. Reynolds is full of praise for what he calls Gainsborough's 'powerful impression of nature' and the 'interesting simplicity and elegance of his little ordinary beggar children'. Yet Reynolds is well aware that his preference for Gainsborough's 'low' subjects, as opposed to the 'great historical stile' practised by the Italian Masters will arouse the censure of other Academic painters. He tries to wriggle out of his own ambivalent position by adding an apology:

> But we have the sanction of all mankind in preferring genius in a lower rank of art, to feebleness and insipidity in the highest.

Figure 52 Thomas Gainsborough, *The Market Cart*, 1786–87, oil on canvas, 183 × 153 cm (72 × 60¼ ins). The Tate Gallery, London.

In writing this tribute, Reynolds must have had in mind later works such as the Tate Gallery *Market Cart*, 1786 (fig 52) in which the loose manner of painting, the atmospheric light and the warm autumnal colours suggest an idyllic rural scene. In Reynolds' eyes, Gainsborough had transformed a common subject into something elegant and appealing.

The key to Reynolds' appreciation can also be found in his own paintings. Despite his views on the superiority of the 'Grand Manner', he too was prone to indulge in 'Ornamental' painting, as in his portrait of Nelly O'Brien, 1760–62 (fig. 53). The sensitive use of colours, highlights and surface textures in Nelly O'Brien's dress is, in fact, in harmony with Gainsborough's reply to Mr Hoare, when he praises the 'Ornamental' style of portrait painting.

Figure 53 Joshua Reynolds, *Portrait of Nelly O'Brien*, 1763, oil on canvas. The Wallace Collection, London, reproduced by permission of the Trustees.

2 The Early Landscapes

English landscape painting in the early eighteenth century was dominated by two broad categories: idealized pseudo-classical landscapes in the manner of Claude or Rosa, and topographical views (that is, direct copies of specific scenes) as illustrated in the works of Paul Sandby (fig 54).[27]

Figure 54 Paul Sandby, *Distant View of Leith*, 1747, watercolour and pencil. Ashmolean Museum, Oxford.

Gainsborough's landscapes do not fit easily into either category, although a letter to Lord Hardwicke, probably of about 1764, after he had moved to Bath, would seem to indicate a preference for the classical style of landscape painting:

> With respect to real Views from Nature in this country he [Gainsborough] has never seen any place that affords a subject equal to the poorest imitations of Gaspar and Claude. Paul Sandby is the only Man of Genius, he believes, who has employed his Pencil that way. Mr. G. hopes Lord Hardwicke will not mistake his meaning, but if his Lordship wishes to have anything tolerable of the name of G., then the subject altogether, as well as the figures etc must be of his own Brain.
>
> Woodall, no 87, p. 91

Gainsborough implies that he has never attempted to emulate Sandby's style, informing Lord Hardwicke that he prefers to use his imagination when working out a subject.

In 1748 Gainsborough did, however, paint one notable work in the topographical style: the *Charterhouse* (fig 55) for the governor's courtroom of the Foundling Hospital. At the time he was studying under Gravelot, a French engraver associated with the St Martin's Lane School, and in this environment he became familiar with the work of several French rococo engravers working in London.[28] He was also exposed to the anti-establishment ideas for which the St Martin's Lane group, which included the painter and engraver William Hogarth, became renowned (see Unit 7).

[27] Other well-known artists working in the topographical style included Samuel Scott and Samuel Wale. Paul Sandby was also an engraver and a member of the Royal Academy. He launched a vendetta against Hogarth's *Analysis of Beauty* which he attacked in a series of satirical prints.

[28] In this environment Gainsborough got to know the work of Mercier and engravings by the French painter Watteau (see Unit 30). While working as Gravelot's assistant he probably worked directly on some of the rococo portrait heads attributed to his master. (See J. Hayes, *The Drawings of Thomas Gainsborough* (1970), Zwemmer, p. 55.)

Figure 55 Thomas Gainsborough, *The Charterhouse* 1748, oil on canvas, 56 cm (22 ins) diameter. Thomas Coram Foundation for Children, London.

The *Charterhouse* probably owes something to Hogarth's influence in the use of sharply receding perspective lines (see Unit 7), and in the ordinariness of the subject matter. There is also a strong rococo influence in the decorative circular frame, a device often used by French eighteenth-century painters and engravers. (In painting, as in architecture, the term rococo is used to describe a decorative style, often based on the shell motif and 's' shaped rhythms—see p. 16.)

More typical of Gainsborough's early landscape style are the works inspired by the Suffolk countryside (plate 4). In 1748, two years after his marriage to Margaret Burr, he returned to his native Suffolk village of Sudbury to earn his living as a painter. John Hayes has neatly summarized Gainsborough's favourite subjects from this period:

> Chiefly woodland scenes, with pools or streams, winding tracks, knolls with sandy or chalky banks, cottages nestling among trees and church towers rising over them. Shepherd boys with flocks of sheep, drovers and cattle, plough-teams, woodgatherers, milkmaids, herdsmen resting (or sleeping) beside a path, cows silhouetted on banks, and groups of donkeys were introduced to diversify the landscape, and ploughshares and withered or pollarded trees, especially the latter, which lent themselves so readily to rococo treatment, were also familiar motifs.
>
> *The Drawings of Thomas Gainsborough*, p. 48

This rural subject matter, largely inspired by the 'common nature' which he saw around him in Suffolk, was the antithesis of Reynolds' learned historical style. Bate Dudley, in Gainsborough's obituary in the Morning Herald of 1788, has suggested that Gainsborough's artistic education was derived entirely from nature: 'Nature was his teacher and the woods of Suffolk his Academy' (*The Morning Herald*, 4 August 1788).

Exercise

Please look at the works from Gainsborough's Suffolk period that are included in this unit—the *Study of Burdock Leaves* (fig 56), the *River Scene with Figures and Dog Barking at a Swallow* (fig 50) and Gainsborough's *Forest* (plate 4). To what extent could these works be called 'naturalistic' in the sense of a direct copy from nature? How is this reflected in the style of these works?

Figure 56 Thomas Gainsborough, *Study of Burdock leaves*, late 1740s, black chalk, 14 × 18.5 cm ($5\frac{1}{2} \times 7\frac{1}{4}$ ins). Reproduced by permission of the Trustees of the British Museum.

Discussion

The *Burdock Leaves* is clearly a study from nature, but even in this early drawing we can identify the more personal characteristics of Gainsborough's style. The shading follows the strong diagonal rhythms that dominate later drawings and there is an emphasis on undulating, serpentine lines in the shapes of the leaves.

In the *River Scene* there is a similar emphasis on serpentine rhythms (probably influenced by rococo sources which were familiar to Gainsborough from the St Martin's Lane environment) in the lines of the paths, the trees and the general sense of an irregular, meandering landscape.

You might also have noticed the way in which the groups of figures and animals are used in both paintings to break open spaces or add to the visual interest. Gainsborough's 'little dirty subjects' have an important compositional role to play. They create, in his own words, 'a little business for the Eye to be drawn from the trees in order to return to them with more glee' (Woodall, no 49, p. 99).

In both paintings, rococo influences are difficult to distinguish from Dutch influences. Most of Gainsborough's biographers have claimed that he would have had access to Dutch works by seventeenth-century painters such as Ruisdael (1628–82), Hobbema (1638–1709), Waterloo (1610–90) and Teniers (1582–1649) in the possession of wealthy East Anglian collectors, and around 1740 many Dutch works were beginning to appear in the London art market.

Gainsborough's *Forest* is very close in composition and treatment of the trees to an earlier drawing (fig 57) which he executed after Ruisdael's *Forest*. The drawing is executed in black and white chalks, a medium which was well suited to evoke the atmospheric effects which Gainsborough clearly admired in Ruisdael's painting.

Figure 57 Thomas Gainsborough, *Wooded Landscape with River, Cattle and Figures* (after Jacob van Ruisdael), 1747, pencil and black chalk, 40.5 × 42 cm (16 × 16½ ins). Whitworth Art Gallery, Manchester.

The term 'naturalistic' is often applied to the works of the Dutch seventeenth-century school for the same reason that it is used to describe Gainsborough's Suffolk style. The Dutch landscape painters listed above generally chose subjects based on the local countryside, avoiding historical or allegorical themes. But this does not mean to say that the rich foliage and the twisted withered trees of Gainsborough's *River Scene* or Ruisdael's *Forest* are exact imitations of a local scene; they are more often features which the artist has exaggerated in the interest of the aesthetic design of the composition as a whole. As Gainsborough wrote in 1764: '. . . anything tolerable of the name of Mr. G. . . must be of his own Brain'.

There is, however, a work from this period which includes a closer imitation of a local Suffolk scene: the portrait of *Mr and Mrs Robert Andrews*, 1748–49, in the National Gallery, London (plate 3). Gainsborough was commissioned to paint the newly married couple in their own grounds, and the portrait group, which occupies less than one half of the total composition, is no more important than the detailed landscape setting. The Andrews' estate (called the Auberies, just outside Sudbury) stretches out into the distance. Gainsborough has painted the couple in relation to their property. Mrs Andrews' rich satin dress, Mr Andrews' squire-like pose with a gun and a faithful dog, and their fertile estate abundant with freshly harvested sheaves of corn all contribute to an image of proud and affluent landowners.

I think that it is important to see this sort of portrait as a reflection of both Gainsborough's taste for landscape painting and the significance of patronage in his work. In the same way that an eighteenth-century patron would commission a house in a style which he believed was best suited to express his own importance the Andrews commissioned a portrait that demonstrated the extent of their estate and their importance as landowners.[29]

This may be a reason why *Mr and Mrs Robert Andrews* is one of the Suffolk works which comes closest to a 'naturalistic' study of a specific place. Although we can never know, of course, exactly what their estate looked like, the enclosed fields, the sheep and the church spire have a note of authenticity about them. They are relatively free of the rococo serpentine lines that characterize Gainsborough's *Forest* or his *River Scene*.

[29] A similar argument has been developed by John Berger in *Ways of Seeing* (1972), Penguin, p. 107. He has emphasized what he calls the Andrews' 'proprietory attitude towards what surrounds them'.

3 The Bath Period

In 1759 Gainsborough and his family moved from Ipswich to Bath, where he hoped to find a more lucrative source of commissions. In this fashionable upper-class resort he began to establish a reputation as a portraitist with a talent for capturing a good likeness. (This talent was encouraged during his early links with the St Martin's Lane set and the example of Hogarth.) Commissions increased and by 1766 he could afford to move into a house in the recently built Circus.

During this period there are noticeable changes in Gainsborough's landscape style. Influenced by an environment in which many wealthy collectors were accumulating seventeenth-century Italian and French masterpieces, he began to evolve his own personal 'grand style'.

Gainsborough's praise of the work of Gaspar Poussin and Claude in his letter to Lord Hardwicke takes on more relevance during this period. Many of the Bath landscapes use a compositional form which may have been derived from French seventeenth-century works. In, for instance, the *River Landscape with Figures in a Boat*, 1768–70 (plate 5) he follows a rather Claudean composition in the arrangement of the figure group in the foreground which is framed by river banks and trees.

A more important influence on Gainsborough's style in the 60s and 70s was the work of Sir Peter Paul Rubens (1577–1640). In the fourteenth *Discourse* Reynolds comments that Gainsborough had made copies from Rubens' paintings, and in a letter of 1768 to the actor David Garrick, Gainsborough mentions 'His Grace's [the Duke of Montagu] Landskip of Rubens' (Woodall, no 27, p. 67). He was referring to the *Watering Place* (fig 58) now in the National Gallery, London.

Gainsborough later painted his own *Watering Place* (plate 6) which was exhibited at the Royal Academy in 1777 and caused Horace Walpole to scribble in the margin of his exhibition catalogue: 'In the style of Rubens, and by far the finest landscape ever painted in England and equal to the great Masters' (Quoted by John Hayes in 'Gainsborough and Rubens', *Apollo*, August 1963, p. 92).

Exercise

Please look carefully at Rubens' *Watering Place* (fig 58) and Gainsborough's painting of the same title (plate 6). Are there any similarities in the style and composition of these works? Why do you think Walpole showed such enthusiasm for Gainsborough's painting?

Discussion

As Walpole suggests, Gainsborough had absorbed many elements from Rubens' style. The subject matter, the dark trees with heavy roots and loosely painted leaves, the highlighted group of drinking animals and the general composition in which a central group is framed with trees are features which echo the Duke of Montagu's painting. However, there are several differences in the details of the two compositions. The figures and the animals appear to be more dispersed in the Rubens. Gainsborough's arrangement is more compact and the central group is more obviously enclosed by the trees.

One could also argue that Gainsborough, like Rubens, has tended to idealize the scene. In both works the light atmospheric treatment of the leaves, the highlighted central group and the general air of calm, help to evoke a scene of pastoral contentment.

I think that in Gainsborough's *Watering Place* Walpole found a style and composition which satisfied both his taste for the great seventeenth-century masters

Figure 58 Sir Peter Rubens, *The Watering Place*, 1615–17, oil and black chalk on wood, 99 × 134.5 cm (39 × 53 ins). London, the National Gallery.

and his ideas on 'modern' gardening. The sheltered hollow set against a gentle hill was not far removed from Walpole's 'delicious contrast of hill and valley changing imperceptibly into each other' . . . and . . . 'the beauty of the gentle swell or concave swoop'. Similarly, the sturdy trees with their broad areas of loosely painted foliage reminds one of Walpole's comments on Kent's activities when 'the living landscape was not chastened or polished . . . Freedom was given to the forms of the trees; they extended their branches unrestricted' (Course Anthology Vol 2).

The Barber Institute *Harvest Wagon* from the late 1760s (plate 7) is a work from the Bath period which also suggests the influence of Rubens. This can be seen in the use of highlights on the central group of peasants, the large trees which frame the central group (although this pictorial device could also be derived from Claude) and the broad handling of the leaves.

What is striking in this painting is the way in which the figures and the horses create a strong sense of diagonal movement; the figures on the cart form a triangular group which seems to be pushing laterally across the canvas. This pyramid of figures is now recognized as a quotation from the central group in Rubens' *Descent from the Cross* in Antwerp Cathedral (fig 59). Gainsborough was probably working from one of the many engraved copies of the altarpiece that were available in England at the time.

Figure 59 Sir Peter Paul Rubens, *Descent from the Cross*, 1611, panel, 114.5 × 76 cm (45 × 30 ins); original design for the Antwerp painting. London, Courtauld Institute Galleries, Lee Collection.

Under the influence of Rubens, Gainsborough painted the *Harvest Wagon* in a more generalized style than his earlier Suffolk landscapes. In the *Harvest Wagon* there is less attention to detail; the emphasis is on an all-pervading atmosphere rather than the particular characteristics of each motif. In a sense, Gainsborough could be seen to be developing his own 'grand style'.

The move to Bath gave Gainsborough the opportunity to observe several recently laid-out gardens in the area, such as Ralph Allen's gardens at Prior Park (these are discussed in television programme 2 on Bath) which were much admired by Fielding in *Tom Jones* (p. 545), and Capability Brown's adaptation of the grounds at Longleat. Gainsborough's now destroyed *Portrait of Garrick* of 1766 (fig 60) suggests that he may have been influenced by developments in landscape gardening. The actor David Garrick, who was one of Gainsborough's closest friends, is shown with one arm around a bust of Shakespeare. The background, which includes an ornamental Palladian bridge, has been identified by Walpole as Prior Park. If the setting *is* Prior Park then this is Capability Brown's unfinished Palladian bridge. Like the bust of Shakespeare, the bridge may have been included as a reference to Garrick's personal interests. But it seems more likely that Gainsborough was merely including in his portrait a fashionable piece of decoration which he had observed in a local 'modern' garden.

Figure 60 Thomas Gainsborough, *David Garrick*, 1766 (destroyed by fire at Stratford on Avon Town Hall, 1946), oil on canvas, 245 × 152.5 cm ($92\frac{1}{2} \times 60$ ins). Photograph from E. Waterhouse *Gainsborough* (1958), Edward Hulton, London, plate 86. Reproduced by kind permission of Sir Ellis Waterhouse.

4 The Later Landscapes: 'An Ideal Common Life'

In 1774 Gainsborough returned to London, settling with his family in Schomberg House, Pall Mall. Between this time and his death in 1788 he continued to paint landscapes, although they rarely attracted buyers. He regularly sent landscapes to the Royal Academy exhibitions (the 1780 exhibition included as many as six) in the hope that the public would recognize the merit of this part of his oeuvre.

Despite his new proximity to the Academy, he continued to avoid historical subjects (apart from two exceptions, *Hagar and Ishmael* and *Diana and Acteon* both in the Buckingham Palace collection), preferring portraits and a wide range of rustic subjects. The latter included simple landscapes, landscapes with peasant groups and the so-called 'fancy pictures'. The category of 'fancy pictures' was first used by Reynolds in the fourteenth *Discourse* to describe Gainsborough's portraits of unsophisticated country people such as shepherds, woodmen, children minding animals and courting peasants (figs 61 and 62).

Figure 61 Thomas Gainsborough, *Woodcutter Courting a Milkmaid*, 1755, oil on canvas, 111 × 129.5 cm ($43\frac{3}{4}$ × 51 ins). Reproduced by kind permission of the Marquess of Tavistock and the Trustees of the Bedford Estates.

Figure 62 Thomas Gainsborough, *Haymaker and Sleeping Girl*, *c* 1785, oil on canvas, 226 × 148.5 cm (89 × 58½ ins). Boston, Museum of Fine Arts.

In a review published in *The Champion* on 31 July 1814, William Hazlitt made some perceptive comments about these works:

> It is, perhaps, the general fault of Gainsborough, that he presents us with an ideal common life, of which we have had a surfeit in poetry and romance. His subjects are softened and sentimentalized too much; it is not simple unaffected nature that we see, but nature sitting for her picture. Our artist, we suspect led the way to that masquerade by giving the air of an Adonis to the driver of a hay cart.

Although Hazlitt is, perhaps, overstating his case in the reference to Adonis, Gainsborough's fancy pictures often present peasants as innocent and sentimentalized creatures who inhabit a rustic arcadia, reflecting a Rousseauistic approach to the countryside and its inhabitants.[30]

[30] Similar idealized attitudes towards nature and the virtues of rural life can also be found in the work of several contemporary poets. For example, in James Thomson's poem 'The Seasons' (1726–30) there is a similar sentiment for nature and rustic scenes. The relationship between poetry and painting in the mid eighteenth century is discussed in C. B. Tinker *Painter and Poet*, (1938), Harvard.

In, for instance, the *Haymaker and Sleeping Girl* of *c* 1785 (fig 62) the generalized style of the foliage and the hazy sunlit landscape between the figures, contribute to an all-pervading softened atmosphere. As Hazlitt suggests, we are led to suspect that nature has been posed for her picture. This sense of an idealized, 'painted' nature anticipates the taste for 'picturesque' landscape which became fashionable at the end of the eighteenth century. Gainsborough formed a friendship with Uvedale Tomkyns Price, the father of the better known Uvedale Price whose *Essays on the Picturesque* appeared in 1794. Gainsborough's own aesthetic preferences in later life were probably influenced by ideas popular in the Price circle. In volume 2 of his *Essays on the Picturesque* (1810), the younger Price recalls Gainsborough's reactions when he accompanied them on riding trips in the country:

> When we came to cottage or village scenes, to groups of children, or to any subjects of that kind which struck his fancy, I have often remarked in his countenance an expression of particular gentleness and complacency.

When he painted his cottage scenes this 'feeling of gentleness' was transferred onto the canvas. In the *Woodcutter's Return*, *c* 1773 (fig 63) he presents us with a peaceful scene of rural life in which a loving and disturbingly healthy-looking family await the return of the toiling woodcutter. The cosy little cottage, nestled amongst the trees, is a warm, inviting place in which to end the day's work. In this work

Figure 63 Thomas Gainsborough, *The Woodcutter's Return*, *c* 1773, oil on canvas, 147.5 × 122 cm (58 × 48 ins). Belvoir Castle, Duke of Rutland Collection; photograph Layland Ross Ltd, Nottingham.

Gainsborough's idyllic conception of rural life is inseparable from the variety of visual forms which make up the composition. The highlighted figure group contrasts with the shadowy figure of the woodcutter, and the simple lines of the thatched cottage are broken by the irregular lines of the gnarled tree, creating a 'picturesque' scene.

But what, exactly, was meant by the term the 'picturesque' in the late eighteenth century?

It signified much more than the modern idea of suitable for a picture. Price saw it as an alternative category to the 'Sublime' and the 'Beautiful', categories that were formalized in Burke's *Inquiry into the Origin of our Ideas on the Sublime and the Beautiful*, 1751. Its main characteristics were 'roughness and sudden variation joined to irregularity', and this could mean variations in colour, form and lighting.[31] It provided a means of defining objects which were neither 'Beautiful' (in the sense of pleasing or perfectly formed objects) nor 'Sublime' (In the sense of frightening or likely to arouse the passions). It was used to describe scenes with a primarily *visual*, rather than literary, appeal.

Figure 64 Thomas Gainsborough, *The Cottage Door*, exhibited 1780, oil on canvas, 147.5 × 119.5 cm (58 × 47 ins). San Marino, USA, Henry E. Huntington Library and Art Gallery.

31 The eighteenth century concept of the 'Picturesque' is discussed at length in C. Hussey's book *The Picturesque* (1927), Putnam.

Figure 65 Thomas Gainsborough, *Mountain Landscape with Shepherd and Sheep*, *c* 1783, chalk drawing, 25.5 × 35.5 cm (10 × 14 ins). Puerto Rico, Museo de Arte de Ponce, Fundacion Luis A. Ferre.

Exercise

Please look at *The Cottage Door* 1780 (fig 64) and two later landscape drawings, *Landscape with Shepherd and Sheep*, *c* 1783 (fig 65) and the *Wooded Landscape with Castle*, 1787–88 (fig 66). To what extent do these works anticipate 'picturesque' characteristics?

Discussion

I expect you will have noticed that *The Cottage Door* is very similar in subject matter to the *Woodcutter's Return*. A healthy peasant family, dominated by a rather aristocratic-looking mother, is grouped in front of the cottage door. As in the *Woodcutter's Return* Gainsborough highlights the figure group to create an irregular lighting effect, and the foreground of *The Cottage Door* is dominated by a 'picturesque' variation in the form of a dead tree trunk. In fact, the whole painting has a general quality of roughness and variation, emphasized by the loosely painted leaves and the diagonal movement and counter-movement in the trees and the cottage roof.

In the two drawings, Gainsborough uses the chalk medium to create what Reynolds might have called a 'variety of effect'. In these drawings he was clearly concerned with suggestion rather than detailed descriptions. The *Landscape with Shepherd and Sheep* was inspired by a visit to the Lake District in the summer of 1783, and it is possible that this drawing was executed on the spot. The hills create a sense of diagonal movement which is heightened by the white chalk highlights, and there are strong contrasts (of which Price would surely have approved) between the light and shadowed areas.

Figure 66 Thomas Gainsborough, *Wooded Landscape with Castle*, *c* 1787–8, black and white charcoal with stump on blue laid paper, 26.5 × 33 cm ($10\frac{1}{2}$ × 13 ins). Yale Center for British Art, Paul Mellon Collection, New Haven, Connecticut.

While sharing many of these characteristics the more loosely-sketched *Wooded Landscape* introduced a typical 'picturesque' motif in the ruined castle.[32] The theme of the ruin, often set against dark woods, recurs in Gainsborough's landscape drawings and like his bleak mountain peaks, often evokes an air of melancholy seclusion. In this respect, Gainsborough's landscape drawings can be seen to reflect many of the fashionable aesthetic preoccupations of his time. False ruins were sometimes included in eighteenth-century gardens (as, for example, at Stowe and Shughborough), where they were designed to create an interesting vista and suggest an atmosphere of melancholy and gloom.

The grotto was also a common feature of many gardens from the period (fig 41). It was usually a secluded retreat in the midst of nature—perhaps a cave or a rocky pool—and a place for private contemplation. Pope would often retire to his grotto at Twickenham to indulge in private contemplation. Gainsborough's cosy little cottages, half hidden in dark shadows and sheltered by trees, are indirectly related to the then fashionable idea of a secluded grotto.

There is a more direct relationship in the unfinished painting of *Diana and Acteon* of 1784–85 (fig 67). The setting is from Book 3 of Ovid's *Metamorphoses* and this was one of the rare occasions on which Gainsborough attempted a mythological scene. While out hunting, Acteon discovers Diana and her nymphs bathing. In the painting hc is looking down at the group in the pond while Diana throws the water which will transform him into a horned stag.

32 The contemporary vogue for ruins is well illustrated in the works of the illustrator, the Rev William Gilpin, who also wrote a *Dialogue upon the Gardens at Stowe*.

Figure 67 Thomas Gainsborough. First of three studies for *Diana and Acteon, c* 1784–5, black chalk and grey-black washes on buff paper, 25.5 × 33 cm (10 × 13 ins). Reproduced by courtesy of the Marchioness of Anglesey (Plâs Newydd) and Phaidon Press, Oxford.

Figure 68 Thomas Gainsborough, *Diana and Acteon, c* 1784–5, oil on canvas, 159 × 188 cm ($62\frac{1}{2}$ × 74 ins). Reproduced by kind permission of Her Majesty the Queen.

Diana and Acteon illustrates the way in which in later works Gainsborough would skilfully integrate his figures with their landscape setting. The trees, tree trunks and the rocky banks of the pool occupy the greater part of the canvas, and the lines of the nymphs' bodies echo those of the banks. Similarly, in the first sketch for this work (fig 68) the diagonal lines of both the figures *and* the surrounding trees are used to suggest the drama of movement, in this case the drama provoked by Acteon's unexpected appearance on the scene.

Conclusion

In the fourteenth *Discourse* Reynolds claims that before painting a landscape, Gainsborough would assemble objects in his studio which included:

> Stumps of trees, weeds and animals of various kinds . . . He even framed a kind of model of landskips, on his table, composed of broken stones, dryed herbs, and pieces of looking glass, which he magnified and improved into rocks, trees, and water.
>
> Course Anthology Vol 2, p. 93

Gainsborough selected and rearranged elements from nature which corresponded to the ideas which were 'of his own Brain', creating scenes which were full of incident and visual interest.

Although it seems unlikely that Gainsborough was consciously following contemporary fashions in landscape gardening, similar principles were adopted by the designers of many eighteenth century gardens. Despite their differences, Pope, Kent and Capability Brown constructed their gardens like paintings, balancing areas of light and shade, breaking up monotonous lawns with groups of trees and creating animated vistas. And just as Kent saw 'that all nature was a garden', Gainsborough sought the inspiration for his landscapes in the irregular forms of 'common nature'.

Selected bibliography

(Many of the books listed in the bibliography to Part 1 are relevant to Part 2)

J. Hayes *Gainsborough* (1975), Phaidon. A useful monograph with notes on individual pictures.

J. Hayes *The Drawings of Thomas Gainsborough* (1970), Zwemmer.

J. Hayes 'Gainsborough's Early Landscapes in *Apollo*, 1962, p. 667; 'Gainsborough & Rubens' in *Apollo*, 1963, p. 89; 'Gainsborough's Later Landscapes' in *Apollo*, 1964, p. 20; 'English Painting and the Rococo' in *Apollo*, 1969, p. 114. A series of excellent articles on the development of Gainsborough's landscapes.

J. D. Hunt *The Figure in the Landscape: Poetry, Painting and Gardening in the Eighteenth Century* (1978), John Hopkins University Press. A complex book which attempts to see landscape gardening in a broad intellectual context.

C. Hussey *English Gardens and Landscapes 1700–1750* (1967)

C. Hussey *The Picturesque* (1927), Putnam.

R. Paulson *Emblem and Expression: Meaning in English Art of the Eighteenth Century* (1975), Thames & Hudson. Chapters 1, 2, 6 and 12 are of special interest.

E. K. Waterhouse *Gainsborough* (1958), Edward Hulton. A standard monograph on Gainsborough.

W. T. Whitely *Thomas Gainsborough* (1915), London. An early anecdotal record of Gainsborough's life.

M. Woodall *The Letters of Thomas Gainsborough* (1963), Cupid. Essential reading for a full understanding of Gainsborough's theoretical views.

M. Woodall *Gainsborough's Landscape Drawings* (1939), Faber.

A204 The Enlightenment

Units 1–2	*Tom Jones* by Henry Fielding Part One
Unit 3	Alexander Pope's *An Essay on Man* (Epistle IV)
Units 4–5	*Tom Jones* by Henry Fielding Part Two
Unit 6	Architecture and Landscape
Unit 7	William Hogarth
Units 8–9	Hume's *Enquiry concerning the Principles of Morals*
Units 10–12	Gibbon's *The Decline and Fall of the Roman Empire*
Units 13–14	The *Encyclopédie*
Units 15–16	Frederick the Great
Units 17–18	Buffon's *Natural History*
Units 19–20	*Candide* by Voltaire
Units 21a–24a	Haydn in London
Unit 21b–24b	Mozart's *The Marriage of Figaro*
Units 25–27	Adam Smith's *Wealth of Nations*
Unit 28	Hume's Essays on Miracles and Providence
Unit 29	French Architecture
Unit 30	Chardin
Units 31–32	*Dangerous Acquaintances* by Choderlos de Laclos